Tony — For

With

Tropical Marine Aquaria

Tropical Marine Aquaria
The Natural System

by
R. A. Riseley

LONDON
GEORGE ALLEN & UNWIN LTD
RUSKIN HOUSE MUSEUM STREET

FIRST PUBLISHED IN 1971

ISBN 0 04 639002 2

PRINTED IN GREAT BRITAIN
in 11 on 13 point Times Roman
BY COX & WYMAN LTD
FAKENHAM

To the memory of Molly Riseley

Acknowledgements

I am most grateful to the various experts and friends who have helped me with encouragement, advice, identification of specimens or other assistance, especially:

> Dr Lev Fishelson of the Department of Zoology, Tel Aviv University
>
> Mr R. E. Sharma of the Department of Zoology, Singapore University
>
> Mr Peter Whitehead of the British Museum (Natural History)

Permission to use the photograph facing page 32 was kindly given to me by Mr Larry Harris and I am indebted to the Tong Photo Service of Singapore for much patience and skill in taking all the other colour photographs in this book except those credited to me.

My thanks are also due to the Department of External Affairs, Canberra and to the Smithsonian Institute, Washington, for providing copies of works now out of print.

The Librarians of the University of Singapore, British Museum (Natural History) and Royal Zoological Society have been most helpful in allowing me to consult reference books.

Permission to quote from copyright material (the sources of which are acknowledged in the text) has been granted by the following:

> Holt, Rinehart and Winston, Inc., of New York (Marine Botany: *An Introduction,* by E. Yale Dawson)
>
> The Trustees of the British Museum (Natural History) (Great Barrier Reef Expedition 1928–9 Scientific Reports)
>
> Dr Lev Fishelson (*Bulletin of the Sea Fish Research Station, Haifa and Israel Journal of Zoology.*)

Mr C. van Duijn Jnr not only allowed me to make use of information contained in his book *Diseases of Fishes* (2nd edn, Iliffe Books Ltd., London, 1967) but helped most generously by reading through and suggesting revisions to my section on fish diseases.

Finally, and above all, my thanks are due to Mr Lee Chin Eng of Djakarta who introduced me to the 'natural' system and to Mr Derek McInerny, the 'friend in England' referred to throughout the text.

Contents

Illustrations

ONE COLOUR *between pages* 96–97

1 & 2.   A species of Euphyllia

3 & 4. *Polyphyllia talpina*

5. *Pectinia lactuca*

6. *Herpolitha limax*

7 & 8.   *Podabacia crustacea*

9.   Coral of the *Merulina* species

10. *Fungia echinata*

11. *Oulastrea crispata*

12. Coral *Acropora*

13. *Merulina ampliata*

14. Crater shaped coral

15. *Favia* sp.

16. Unidentified coral

17. *Dendrophyllia nigrescens*

18. *Favia*

19. *Favites abdita*

20. *Goniopora* sp.

21. *Platygyra lamellina*

22. *Platygyra lamellina*

23. *Goniastrea sp.*

24. *Lobophyllia hemprichii*

Introduction

Mr Lee Chin Eng of Djakarta introduced me to the 'natural' system of marine fish keeping many years ago. This book is an attempt to share the pleasure which we – my wife and I – have experienced in practising the system for ourselves here in Singapore during the past few years.

During Confrontation we were cut off from Mr Lee and had to proceed on our own, with little more than the knowledge that the system could be made to work. We then found out just how little information – other than that of a strictly technical nature – was available to aquarists interested in keeping marine creatures other than fishes and the idea of this book was born at that time. In writing it, our one rule has been to deal only with creatures which we know from personal experience and we have not aimed to provide more than an introduction to the basic principles.

Many of these principles have been known to scientists for some time. For example, the oxygen-generating property of corals was described by Dr J. Verwey forty years ago and the great Barrier Reef Expedition of 1928–9 similarly provided most valuable data. All that is new is that certain facts have been considered in a different context. The conclusions drawn from them may perhaps be unfamiliar to some aquarists.

The term 'natural system' is a misnomer. The system is no nearer to reality than a well-lighted, well-planted freshwater tank is to a leaf-filled jungle pool. It is impossible to simulate the action of the tides or storms, but given a reasonable resemblance to their normal surroundings and a small cross-section of other marine life, many coral fishes will readily adapt themselves to captivity, retaining their full colour and natural behaviour.

Most marine creatures are healthiest when living in association with others. In 'natural' tanks corals, anemones, starfish, tube worms, shrimps, cowries, sea squirts, sea urchins and many other animals – even some plants – will flourish.

There are of course limitations. Many of the sponges will not tolerate tank conditions and some corals, especially arborescent ones, will die. Members of the Chaetodontidae family will eat certain types of coral, trigger fish will peck at tube worms, butterfly fish will kill clams, etc., but,

15

careful selection of specimens should avoid such problems. Guidance on these points is given in the chapters concerned.

Any experienced aquarist who follows the methods recommended should find it possible to set up and maintain marine tanks, but this is not to say that we have reached the final state of the art. There is still a lot more to be learned. Many animals which we have not tried could probably be included. If you wish to experiment with such creatures, however, you must first study the conditions in which they live, their enemies, neighbours and eating habits. Do not try experiments in your established tank but use a quarantine tank for the purpose.

1. General view of a tank
   Photograph by the author

2. Common clowns *(Amphiprion percula)* in anemone
   Photograph by the author

3. Common clowns (*Amphiprion percula*) with tube worm, anemone, green seaweed (*Halimeda*).

1. The Theory of the Natural System

What is a 'natural' marine tank? In theory this would be an exact replica of a reef with currents and tides, having a full complement of animals, plants and rocks. The 'natural' system does not aim at this, but seeks to reproduce reef conditions only in so far as is necessary to achieve an attractive, well-balanced tank in which the creatures will feel at home and thrive. Our test of success is whether they will feed well, growing and maintaining health and colour. When any of the fishes or other creatures breed, then we know that we are succeeding.

This stage has long since been reached by freshwater aquarists: not by striving after sterile conditions, but by careful selection of plants, rocks and fishes and by care with regard to the temperature and condition of the water.

Why, then, apply a different set of principles to the keeping of marine fishes? We believe that sterile systems, filters and ozonifiers, all destroy essential plankton, bacteria and trace elements, make the task of fish keeping more difficult, less exciting and – in the end – a great deal more expensive. The only artificial aids which we recommend beyond a hydrometer and lighting are simple pumps serving aeration stones. The aim is to give moderate to strong aeration depending upon the size and density of the tank population. This assists oxygenation slightly, as in the case of freshwater tanks, but, more important, it assists to remove ammonia and other waste products in similar volatile form. In temperate climates we should also need heaters with thermostats and a thermometer. Drugs are used to treat fishes which are sick or threatened by an outbreak of disease.

Apart from food, which is dealt with in another chapter, the essentials for a healthy tank are: oxygenators, control of waste products and *harmful* bacteria, maintenance of a reasonable *pH* value, water, light and balance.

We do not seek to destroy bacteria and plankton – these creatures, although invisible to the naked eye, are present in astronomical numbers in seawater, sand and rock. Phytoplankton is a powerful oxygenating agent and bacteria probably the most valuable element of all. The following comments by Dr Yale Dawson in *Marine Botany: An Introduction* graphically describe the importance of bacteria in the overall scheme of marine life:

'The influence of marine bacteria on chemical, geological, and biological phenomena in the sea is of major importance. They are the liberators of mineral nutrients for plants by their decomposition of marine plant and animal residues. They contribute to the regeneration of phosphate in that most important marine cycle; they transform sulphur compounds, oxidize ammonia to nitrate, and in various other ways affect the chemical composition of seawater and bottom deposits. The bacteria themselves are important food for numerous kinds of small marine animals. The distribution of oxygen in the sea is to a considerable extent influenced by their enormous consumption of this gas, probably equal to or greater than that of all other organisms combined. They are significant in the geological changes that they effect in sediments after deposition.'

These facts can be more readily appreciated when it is realized that inshore waters, heavy with nutrients drained off from the land, may support between 50,000 and 400,000 bacteria per millilitre. Marine bacteria are on average smaller than their terrestrial counterparts – the latter do not appear to survive to any extent in the sea. Few types of marine bacteria will harm fishes and other creatures and none is reported as causing disease in man.

Oxygenators. In freshwater tanks plants, provided that they have suitable light, will assist by absorbing carbon dioxide given off by the fishes and at the same time providing oxygen. Aeration has little value as an oxygenator but it is useful in ruffling the surface of the water to extend the area of oxygen exchange between air and water.

In a marine tank oxygen can also be provided by plants (or, more correctly, by algae, as very few of these are rooted forms and most have only holdfasts). A few of the green and red algae have value as oxygenators but most of them suffer from the disadvantage that they are seasonal. The value of the larger brown algae is doubtful, even if you can grow them and most of these are seasonal. There are, however, many useful algae which are not recognizable as such. They are found mostly in green and red encrusting forms on coral rock. These lichen-like algae and other

18

types to be found within living animals or in open water, such as phyto-plankton, could well be more reliable oxygenators than the 'seaweed' types which are more easily recognized but mostly difficult to cultivate.

Zooxanthellae are also valuable oxygenators. These small unicellular plants are found within the body of many coelenterates including almost all of the Madreporarian corals, many of which, at least in the wild, produce more oxygen than they can consume during the hours of day-light. Dr J. Verwey, after extensive studies in the Java Sea, advanced the theory that if this were not so, many of the more secluded reefs would be starved of oxygen, especially during the tropical nights.

We have proved for ourselves that corals are excellent oxygenators by keeping a collection in unaerated water for over a month. Admittedly, they were in open-topped tanks without covers, kept outside in plenty of tropical sunlight.

Even in captivity, we think that coral can be helpful in producing oxygen, not only for itself but also for the other tank animals, provided that it has plenty of light. Nevertheless, some of our very successful tanks have had very little coral: in one case there was none. It must be said, however, that these latter tanks had plenty of algae-covered rock and relatively few fishes or other creatures.

Our final conclusion is that the amount of coral, if any, which is necessary varies according to the amount of oxygen which can be absorbed at the water surface, the oxygen requirements of the other inhabitants, and the extent to which oxygen can alternatively be provided by the use of algae.

Control of waste products and harmful *bacteria.* Uric acid is no problem no matter how long the water remains unchanged, because urination by marine fishes is negligible. In this they differ from their freshwater counterparts whose body liquids are more salty than the surrounding water, so that although they do not drink, new water is constantly flowing *into* their bodies through the skin, gills, mouth, etc. In order to maintain a proper liquid balance freshwater fishes must therefore emit large quantities of urine. Marine fishes are in the reverse position: their body fluids are less salty than the seawater, so that there is a continuous *out-flowing* from them into the sea. They overcome the risk of dehydra-tion by drinking heavily and the excess salts from the water are disposed of by special cells in the gill filaments.

Ammonia and other waste products in volatile form are readily re-moved by aeration and by the action of bacteria.

19

Obviously one has to avoid creating *harmful* bacteria by faulty hygiene and must preserve that which is healthy. Our discovery of the value of preserving bacteria was accidental. A load of sand needed for a new tank was dumped, for want of other accommodation, into a spare tank of seawater then being aerated. We intended to take the sand out again the next day for washing in freshwater. But we then discovered that the seawater was crystal clear and the sand clean and sweet and lacking the faintly unpleasant odour which it usually had after many washings. By cleaning the sand in freshwater we had been destroying useful bacteria and other life and creating only the more harmful forms of bacteria.

This discovery about sand lead us to adopt the same procedure with rocks. We collected a large number from the lower levels of a sandbar, leaving upon them the small green algae and harmless growths but removing sponges and anything else likely to decay. These rocks when taken home virtually filled a 50-gallon tank. We added seawater immediately and gave it strong aeration. One week later the water was still crystal clear and the plankton life, unharried by fishes and corals, was very abundant.

The use of unwashed sand and coral rock seems to be a major help towards the success of a tank, as the minute life therein not only serves to feed creatures such as corals, but the bacteria will dispose of decomposition products and liberate useful nutrients from these wastes. A number of creatures such as sea squirts feed upon bacteria. Sponges can act as filters for waste products but themselves need careful observation. They are unpredictable and if decaying and large enough will contaminate the whole tank.

Regular tank maintenance and care with regard to the quarantining of new specimens is essential.

pH value. In sterile tanks the *pH* value is considered to be critical because fishes will not tolerate a rapid change in *pH*. Since the measurement of this value is never a simple process it is pleasing to report that to date we have found no need to do so. This is probably because our tank layouts use a large amount of dead coral rock as a platform on which to display living specimens of various kinds. Such a large alkaline mass, which is natural to the water, must absorb any excess of acidity and so enable the tanks to remain for years if necessary without a water change. A friend in England to whom we have sent corals and coral rock reported that after twelve months without a water change his tanks showed only 0·2 variation in *pH*.

Water. We use only natural seawater because we believe that the bacteria and plankton content are vital factors for tank health. Tank-generated zooplankton may possibly survive in synthetic seawater for a short while, but it cannot flourish because of the complete absence of phyto-plankton in the artificial product.

Fishes which have been converted to synthetic water by dealers have to be very carefully and gradually re-converted to natural seawater, otherwise they will die. This discovery surprised us.

Chemically there appears to be very little difference in salinity be-tween tropical waters and those bordering European and American coasts. Good results have been achieved by a friend in England to whom we regularly send specimens, using inshore water from the English Channel. With a few exceptions, such as water from the Bitter Lakes around Suez, most seawater is likely to be suitable.

We do not know how long the plankton contained in seawater taken from Northern shores will survive when it is heated to tropical tempera-tures, but however short-lived this influx of new creatures and 'plants' may be, it is likely to be welcome to the tank inhabitants.

In the long term, the bulk of the zooplankton remaining in an estab-lished tank will be that generated by the animals. Reports from England all mention the same types of larger zooplankton which we see in our own tanks, such as minute 'shuttlecocks' in mid-water and tiny 'centi-pedes' on the glass.

The most difficult type of plankton to assess is phytoplankton: the invisible drifting plant-life of the sea. As this is mainly a surface dweller and of simple construction it must be adaptable to extremes of tempera-ture and should survive under tank conditions better than zooplankton, provided that adequate light is available. It is possible that waste animal products within the tank may provide sufficient nutrient salts to maintain a self-generating succession of phytoplankton.

We have had many self-sown creatures grow up in our tanks including all types of tube worms, tunicates, bivalves, univalves, crabs, shrimps, zoanthids. All these creatures have a zooplankton form in which the primary food of many of them is phytoplankton. Some may have been introduced into the water in the later stages of their planktonic phase but we know that others could only have been generated within the tank. Since they could not develop to the adult stage without phytoplankton it follows that at least a limited amount can survive for a considerable time.

The tank water should be maintained at a temperature of 78 to 80 degrees Fahrenheit but most fishes will adapt to changes in either

21

direction. In our outside tanks the temperature frequently goes a lot higher.

If you decide to quarantine your seawater before use it should preferably be kept aerated meanwhile.

Light. Provision of suitable lighting was the last and most difficult of the problems which had to be overcome – first of all in Singapore and later in England.

Most of the corals and other creatures in our tanks come from the littoral or immediately sub-littoral zone. This means that for a number of hours every month the corals are subjected to very strong sunlight, particularly during the periods of the spring tides. We believe that corals, or at least their zooxanthellae, may have a limited capacity for 'storing' sunlight, because during the monsoon periods around Singapore there are many grey days. These coincide with seasonal growths of brown algae which blot out most of the available light from the corals at the edge of the reef flats. There are also many days when really low water only occurs during the hours of darkness. Even so, reef corals probably get as much light during the darkest periods in the wild as they can hope to enjoy in the best-lighted indoor tank. Some ultra-violet light is bound to filter through the cloud layers even on the darkest days.

Our first experience was that corals kept indoors under artificial light tended after a time to turn pale and would ultimately become quite colourless. After this, if left in the same poor light, the flesh would waste away. This was particularly noticeable in corals with fleshy polyps such as *Fungia, Trachyphyllia* and *Favia*.

Corals kept in tanks which receive some direct tropical sunlight daily will retain colour and health almost indefinitely and colour loss if any will affect only those in the darker parts of the tank. Algae generated by the strong light can be a nuisance, particularly the red-brown algae, but fortunately this forms essentially on the glass or rockwork. That on the glass is no problem and the rockwork does not matter; in any event gastropods such as cowries seem to welcome the extra food. It does not grow over corals unless these are in poor health and on the point of wasting.

We have found that corals kept out of doors with long periods of exposure to direct tropical sunshine will thrive and grow remarkably. Algae is no problem except for the necessity to clean the glass. Pale corals from dark indoor tanks will recover their colour if given periods of from six to eight weeks out of doors. If tissue wastage has started, however, no period of such exposure can make good the damage.

The experiences outlined above were repeated with the first trial shipments to England. In the spring and summer the tanks bloomed and maintained their health. A gradual falling-off started in the autumn and by January most of the hard corals had died. Other creatures – clams, tube worms, crabs, fishes, etc. – still maintained their health and it seemed obvious that the decline in light value had struck hardest at the creatures most dependent upon zooxanthellae. On the other hand, the large amounts of natural coral rock, and assorted invertebrates had obviously helped to keep the fishes in good health.

As a result of this decline of the coral in England during the darker months, both the friend to whom we had sent coral and we ourselves consulted lighting experts and carried out experiments. The result of the English experiments and the conclusions reached are covered in the section on Choice of a Tank: *Lights*.

Our own lights are a rather warm yellow, but the experts assure us that the colour is unimportant: it is the wavelength of the light which counts. For a description of the lights which we use, please see the section on Choice of a Tank: *Lights*.

We will repeat the advice given elsewhere: breeding tanks should be only dimly lit so far as artificial light is concerned. Natural non-tropical sunlight is a different matter and there is no need to restrict this, provided that some natural shade is provided in the tank. In tropical climates more caution is necessary and exposure is best limited to several hours daily at the most and this preferably at morning or evening. All tanks kept in the open in the tropics should ideally have an opaque protection overhead to prevent direct sunshine in the heat of the day from falling on to the tank.

Balance. A balance has to be struck between the competing demands of the various living creatures for light, oxygen, food and space: protection must be afforded against concentrations of chemicals from decomposition products and from harmful types of bacteria. Most of the main factors which help to achieve such a balance in the sea are present in our tanks – animal, vegetable and mineral.

We believe that it is impossible to provide such a balance in tanks kept according to the sterile method, as all forms of plankton, bacteria and other intermediate creatures are destroyed by such devices as ozonifiers, power filters and the like, so that there is nothing with which to achieve a balance between the fishes on the one hand and harmful bacteria and chemicals from waste products on the other. The use of chemicals will not redress the balance and any particles of uneaten food become a further hazard. Under these conditions the fishes are vulnerable to disease, lose the will to survive and are unlikely to breed.

Coral rock, corals, algae and sand are the most obvious balancing factors but the unseen populations imported with them are no less essential to the equilibrium of the tank. Once this has been established the inhabitants themselves ensure that the tank does not get out of balance. Various chemical and biological changes must, of course, take place constantly but these will largely counter-balance each other. Only in the event of a major disaster such as the death of a large clam should any urgent intervention be necessary.

Summary

The essentials for a 'natural' tank are:

(*a*) *Oxygenators*

Oxygen from the air is absorbed at the surface of the water but oxygen can also be provided by algae, zooxanthellae (contained in corals, etc.) and phytoplankton.

(*b*) *Aeration*

This has little oxygenating power but helps to remove volatile waste products such as ammonia.

(*c*) *Sand*

Sand is a natural filter and provides a home for worms and other creatures which eat harmful bacteria and waste products. Very fine shingle may be substituted if sand is not available.

(*d*) *Rock*

A high proportion of dead coral rock to take care of the *pH* factor. This rock should preferably be collected from well below the waterline so that it is inhabited by other life. Dried out coral rock from above the waterline may be substituted provided that it has not been chemically treated: this will quickly become re-populated in the tank.

(*e*) *Preservation of unseen populations*

Care must be taken at all times to preserve any non-harmful life inhabiting coral rock, sand and seawater, by putting them in an aerated tank as soon as they are brought home, and thereafter maintaining the aeration.

(*f*) *Water*

This must be natural and uncontaminated. Some experts think that water should be quarantined to avoid introducing disease. A temperature of 78 to 80 degrees Fahrenheit is recommended.

(*g*) *Light*

Exposure to natural sunlight for some hours a day gives the best results. In the the northern hemisphere strong artificial lighting will be essential during winter months. (But see sections on Choice of a Tank : Lights, and Adapting the System to Temperate Climates.)

(*h*) *Equipment*

The only essential equipment is:

Heater/thermostat ⎱ not necessary in
Thermometer   ⎰ tropical climates
Air-pump giving aeration through airstones
Hydrometer
Good lighting

Ozonifiers, power or other filters and similar equipment have no place in 'natural' system tanks, although they may have their uses, along with drugs, in hospital tanks. We suspect that sand filters actually help to preserve a certain amount of useful bacteria in allegedly 'sterile' tanks.

2. Choice of a Tank

Size. Size is largely a matter of personal preference. Our tanks vary greatly as to size and content. The biggest is of 150 gallons capacity and measures 5 feet in length. It permits more imposing layouts than smaller tanks and the keeping of larger specimens, but does not allow greater density of fish per gallon of water. The fish are healthy, but no more so than in tanks of the 2 feet 6 inches long size. A length of less than 2 feet 6 inches is unlikely to give satisfactory results over a long period. We have various theories as to why this is so, but only know for certain that a tank less than 2 feet 6 inches long will be difficult to keep healthy.

Shape. We normally use rectangular tanks and prefer those which give greater width than depth. This allows more space for arrangement and provides a larger water surface for oxygen exchange. One of our most successful tanks, which we still use, is square. The frame is iron, coated with bituminous paint, and it is encased in wood to give a picture frame effect on four sides. All tank walls are of glass. The flat wooden top or lid is removable from the side framework and has two flaps in it which give access to the tank. One or other of these is left open for part of the day in order to provide ventilation. There are two centre compartments within this lid, one of which houses the lights (screened from the water by perspex) and the other contains the aerator. Four tubes from this serve each corner of the tank. Switches in the aerator compartment control the lights and the motor. In temperate climates a further switch would be necessary for the heater and thermostat and some means would have to be found for ventilation other than leaving the flaps open. The electricity supply is by means of one 3-core lead carried in ducting along the floor from a wall point. All screws used in the top are protected against corrosion caused by contact with the water and so are the hinges. This type of tank is very suitable for the central position in a room. It has the virtue of being compact and noise from the aerator motor is muffled.

26

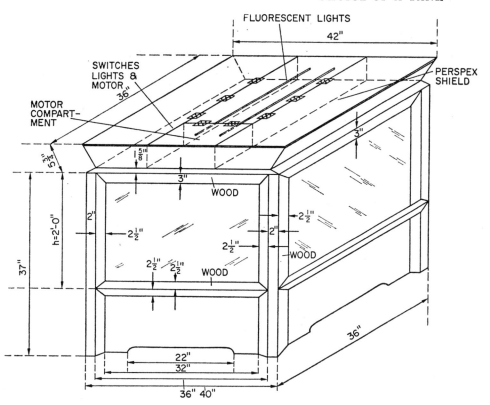

Material and Method of Construction. Metal used for tanks should be non-corrodible: if any other type of metal is used this must be treated to prevent the formation of rust, etc. Whatever the metal and however it is treated it must not come into contact with water which may drip back into the tank and cause metal poisoning. No metal, not even the best stainless steel, should be used for flanges overlapping the inside of the tank. If these are necessary they must be made of other material or designed to jut outwards and slope slightly downwards away from the water. Not all stainless steels are rustproof, many are only rust resistant and the quality of the metal can vary greatly. Check carefully before buying a tank using this material. The best are very good but correspondingly expensive.

Painted, iron-framed tanks are suitable, subject to the above remarks about flanges, and provided that they are coated either with several coats (including undercoat) of good grade marine paint or with a bituminous paint – the latter, however, is normally only obtainable in black.

The most economic and enduring type of tank frame appears to be

27

nylon-coated iron. Although we have not used this type ourselves we have inspected some which have been in continuous service for two years and which do not yet show the faintest specks of rust. The nylon protection appears to be so effective that our earlier advice against overlapping flanges may not apply for this type of tank.

Tanks coated with a tough layer of good quality plastic are likely to have similarly enduring qualities.

A new type of tank employing anodized aluminium is now available. The surfaces more liable to contact with seawater have a thicker top layer. These appear very attractive and are claimed to have given good service over two years. They are, however, considerably more expensive than the nylon-coated tanks.

Perspex and all-glass tanks have no rusting problems but neither material is particularly practical for tanks of the size required for marine work. Perspex is liable to scratching and all-glass tanks, however secure the bonding, do not have the intrinsic strength of a metal-framed tank.

Concrete tanks are widely used in the East for freshwater fishes. They have an inset glass panel in the front and sometimes in the side walls as well. These tanks are inexpensive and satisfactory for a time but later develop rust spots. This happens when the metal with which they are reinforced oxidizes so that the rust works through the concrete to the inner surface of the tank. It works through on the outer surface, too, but that matters less. One of our friends coats such tanks with an epoxy resin which he claims gives very satisfactory results and we intend to try this method. Many of the fish illustrated in this book were photographed in concrete tanks – see especially the illustration of *Amphiprion* with spawn facing page 32.

German aquarists frequently use asbestos tanks. This could be a very suitable and inexpensive medium and the fact that it is popular in Germany, where there are many enthusiastic aquarists, suggests that it is efficient.

To summarize on the best type of tank frame: our first choice would be nylon-coated iron. Stainless steel or anodized aluminium tanks appear to be satisfactory but are very much more expensive. Steel-framed tanks with good protective paint are more economical, but will obviously require more maintenance over the years.

Tank bottoms should ideally be made of glass. Cement can be used, however, and our largest tank has a 3-inch thick concrete floor. In such a case it is essential to ensure that the metal reinforcement is well bedded down. Slate, which is liable to be broken down by seawater, is un-suitable.

When putty or any other glazing medium is used it is necessary to be very careful in choosing the product. Check its suitability with the supplier and reject any putty which is obviously oily or soft. No tank should have putty plainly visible on the inside. Our larger tanks have a layer of cement *over* the putty which is used to fill in the gap between the bottom of the glass wall and the floor of the tank.

Tank covers should preferably be of plastic or of wood and the lights should be screened from the water by glass or perspex. Some types of unscreened fluorescent lights will kill certain creatures.

There must be ample ventilation to prevent undue surface heat and to permit the dispersal of carbon dioxide and various nitrogenous wastes. Lighting is very important but the amount and the quality needed vary with local conditions. We have dealt with this subject in detail in the following section on light.

Lights. Sunlight has been called radiant energy. In the sea as on land most life needs abundant light. Corals, clams and other creatures which rely upon symbiotic plants for full health are found at their most luxuriant growth just below the level of the lowest spring tides. This means that for long periods they receive very strong light and even at the highest tides are rarely more than 20 feet below the surface waters.

Light intensity varies enormously according to the time of day, season and latitude. Clouds will not only cut off a great deal of light when the sky is overcast, but can, at other times, actually intensify it by acting as reflectors.

The angle at which the light strikes the sea is important: when this is oblique there will be loss through reflection back from the surface of the water. Maximum penetration will therefore be greatest in the tropics. Particles of smoke and water vapour will cut down the intensity of the light before it reaches the water. Light penetrating the water surface will again be reduced by the scattering effect of plankton, sediment, etc.

Most of the animals in our tanks come from the sunlit upper waters which enjoy high light penetration, but even these waters very often carry a great deal of sediment, particularly along the fringing reefs and normal light intensity is reduced considerably at monsoon periods. Heavy seasonal growth of brown algae also cuts the light to many corals at some periods of the year. Nevertheless, the total amount of light received

29

over the year in natural conditions in the tropics far exceeds that available in northern latitudes.

For this reason the tropical marine aquarist is in a much more favoured position than is his counterpart in temperate zones.

Given a reasonable degree of direct sunlight, say several hours early morning or evening light each day, most hard corals will flourish for many months if not indefinitely. Full midday sunlight is best limited to short periods, particularly if the tank is small. Should corals and anemones lose colour within a short period of collection the tank must be relocated to permit longer exposure to sunlight. The animals affected will need to be removed to a place where they can get extra daily doses (i.e. higher than would normally be recommended) of natural light, until they recover, as they will do – provided that tissue wastage has not commenced.

For tropical zones we suggest the following lighting which we have used in some of our tanks. Requirements will naturally vary according to the degree of natural light available; we find, however, that the intensity of light recommended gives pleasing results.

Over a 5-foot long tank: Two 40-watt tubes specification TLF 40W/33.*

These are claimed to give 50 per cent more light for the wattage than ordinary tubes. The light is rather yellowish but a bluer one is available under a different catalogue number.

Over a 2-foot 6-inch long tank: Two 20-watt tubes specification TL 20W/ 33T.*

Over a 2-foot 6-inch square tank: Two 20-watt tubes specification TL 20W/32 de luxe.*

Unless the tanks are located in dark places, the lights need not be switched on during the daytime, but will be needed during the evening hours.

In temperate zones little, if any, increase in lighting may be necessary during the summer months but the long dark days of winter will call for greater intensity of light. Without this, hard corals will not survive for even a reasonable period. Provided that the display does NOT include the hard Madreporarian corals or clams, the degree of lighting need not be greater than that recommended for tropical regions. It would, however,

* These are the code numbers allocated by the large Dutch company which makes these lights.

be desirable to keep the lights on all day during the darker months, (Some anemones may lose colour slightly under this degree of lighting as they owe some of their colour to zooxanthellae, but unlike corals or clams anemones do not need to rely upon these to the same extent and will most probably survive if proper feeding is maintained.)

If hard corals are required, then much more light is necessary. It has been suggested by lighting consultants that a light value of 5,000 lumens per square foot be aimed for as a mean average of the normal lighting intensity in tropical regions. This we feel is over-generous as it does not take into account the effect of the scattering action of sediments or variations in weather, tides and other factors such as seasonal weed growths. Dr Yale Dawson has commented that even in clear water only some 35–38 per cent of the sunlight that enters the water penetrates to a depth of one metre.

Experience in England during the past two winters has shown that two 5-foot fluorescent tubes suspended a few feet above two 2-foot 6-inch tanks adjacent to each other were not enough to preserve the Madreporarian corals through the winter – although all other creatures including anemones survived. We feel that if this intensity were doubled even the Madreporarian corals might survive. Practical problems of housing and cooling such a battery of fluorescent tubes are, however, likely to arise. In our view a much more practical solution might be:

Over a 2-foot 6-inch or 3-foot long tank: One 2-foot 6-inch long 20-watt maximum intensity fluorescent tube (which will give a wide spread of light) and four 75-watt incandescent lamps.

This arrangement would allow of more compact housing, but if the lights are to be fitted flush with the tank top precautions must be taken to prevent overheating, particularly of the surface glass and water. With such an intense degree of lighting, do not forget to leave plenty of hiding-places for fish and other mobile creatures: all will flourish better for the good light to which they are accustomed – but even in the wild most coral fish will lurk in dark crannies for some periods and continuous strong light without refuges could harm them.

When incandescent lights are used the resultant algae on glass, etc., are likely to be those of the green type, whereas if fluorescent tubes alone are used the algae are almost invariably of the brown type.

Further work needs to be done on lighting before Madreporarian corals can be expected to survive throughout the long dark days of winter, but

31

it is already possible to keep many of the other creatures through this period and a solution to the problem of the corals may not be too far distant.

We have not attempted to cover the problems of spectral wave-lengths and the degree to which the various colours – violet, green, blue, yellow, red will penetrate water. We did at one time carry out trials with ultra-violet on the verge of the visible spectrum, but found this of little, if any, benefit. It was in fact harmful in some instances. We would not advise further experiments in this sector, save by lighting experts.

Heating and Heaters. Water temperatures should be in the 78 to 80 degrees Fahrenheit zone. In tropical climates this is the natural temperature for a tank located within the house. Outside tanks with too much direct sun may overheat dangerously and the remedy for this is either to re-locate them in a less exposed position or to provide a light-shade screen. Tanks in air-conditioned rooms, in which the temperature is normally about 70 degrees Fahrenheit will require artificial heating. Such rooms are often relatively dark and in this case lighting should also be stepped up close to that recommended for temperate zones.

Heaters will be necessary in temperate zones. Any of those produced by well-known manufacturers are likely to be suitable, but before selecting one make sure that there are no metal parts likely to come into contact with water.

Most heaters are a simple heating coil completely sealed within a strong glass tube. The most common type is controlled by a separate thermostat.

Concerning the location of heaters, the general rules with regard to freshwater tanks apply, i.e. avoid burying heaters in sand or gravel, etc. A few new points arise: do not, for example, locate a heater close to a piece of coral or group of tube worms. Such static creatures cannot move to avoid any uncomfortable local radiation of heat. (The heater when working does, of course, develop a much higher local temperature than the main tank setting.) Fast-moving invertebrates such as bristle worms or shrimps may blunder into heaters and receive damaging burns. Slower moving ones such as cowries or olives may crawl over the heater when it is 'off' and receive fatal burns when it comes 'on'. One solution is to place the heater in a large tube of heat-resistant plastic which has been perforated to allow circulation of water, whilst denying access to the direct heating surface.

4. Breeding cardinal clowns with spawn

own eggs on sixth day
er spawning
otograph by Mr. Larry
rris, taken in our tank

6. Rose clowns *(Amphiprion perideraion)* playing in anemones on an upturned clam shell

7. Blue damsel fish *(Pomacentrus coeruleus)* with coral *(Goniopora)*, fish in cave, small green rock anemones, zoanthids (in right hand corner) and sea squirt. In the centre foreground is a *Trachyphyllia geoffroyi*

Thermostats. The thermostat is incorporated into the same circuit as the heater and most function on the expansion or contraction of a bimetallic strip which bends slightly according to temperature. When the maximum desired temperature is reached, the contacts attached to the strip will snap apart breaking off further supply to the heater. As the water cools the strip will straighten bringing the contact points closer together and, when the minimum permitted temperature is reached they will snap together, thus returning power to the heater – this action is assisted by small magnets incorporated in the points. Thermostats incorporate control knobs to regulate the desired control temperature which is established visually from a separate thermometer within the tank. Once set, the thermostat automatically opens or shuts when the temperature varies more than a few degrees either side of the desired control temperature.

Some of the more modern heaters also incorporate a thermostat which simplifies matters. The basic principle is exactly the same as that of the separate heaters and thermostats. One inconvenience of this combined device is that location is inevitably on the bottom of the tank and adjustments are more lengthy than with the other type where the control thermostats will be above water level. The comments below with regard to the location of the thermometer are just as important for this type of heater-thermostat.

Thermometers. It is important to ensure that the thermometer is not too close to the surface, particularly if powerful lighting is used, as surface water will inevitably be warmer than the main body of water in the tank. A good position is slightly below the middle section of the tank and as far away from the heater as possible, to avoid rising convection currents. If this point is overlooked the main tank water may be considerably cooler than indicated.

A wide range of inexpensive and useful aquarium thermometers is available. The type which we use is circular with an indicating dial. It is completely waterproof and has no exposed metal. Attachment to the tank side is by means of a rubber suction disc.

Although used as a reference when setting the thermostat to give a desired mean temperature – thermometers are not of course in any way physically connected to these pieces of equipment.

Hydrometers. These are basically simple instruments to determine the specific gravity of seawater and thus act as a guide to its salinity. They will not indicate variations in the *types* of salt, but for practical purposes they are a reasonably accurate guide for aquarists.

The hydrometer looks like a clinical thermometer but is somewhat more bulbous and larger. It has a similar graduated scale. The reading is taken where the scale is intercepted by the surface of the water. This should normally be in the region of about 1·025 or even slightly less. Higher readings indicate increases in salinity and freshwater should be added to reduce it accordingly.

A hydrometer should not be left permanently in the water. Dirt and scum can accumulate and assist to give a false reading. It should be kept in a safe place and used when required. Use once a week should be sufficient in any climate. (Anemones resent sudden heavy additions of freshwater and evaporation losses should be made good at frequent intervals.)

Larger hydrometers although more expensive are easier to use and are overall more reliable. If possible, try to secure one calibrated as near as possible to your operating temperature. Some are calibrated at 65 degrees Fahrenheit.

Aeration and Pumps. We have found that simple vibrator pumps are completely satisfactory. We use one of French manufacture which has proved very reliable. Even when a relatively large number of tanks is concerned, it is easier to run extra electrical wiring around the room than to have a maze of small-bore airlines. Air losses due to friction loss in small-bore tubes and from faulty air-lead connection points are also correspondingly reduced.

We prefer medium to strong aeration depending upon the size and density of the tank population. One vibrator pump should be sufficient to serve two 2-foot 6-inch or 3-foot tanks – in some cases it might even suffice for three such tanks if the fish density is low. If high fish densities are required, one of these pumps may be necessary for each tank. As mentioned elsewhere, oxygenation provided by aeration is of relatively little importance. The primary function of the aerator is the disposal of excess carbon dioxide and nitrogenous wastes – these principally emanate from fish. Most of the more sedentary invertebrates do not require strong aeration, but a notable exception to this rule are the larger anemones, which are greedy for it. The degree of aeration necessary for any tanks and the corresponding number of pumps depends mainly upon the required density of the fish and anemone population per tank.

Violent aeration is not desirable at any time and is in any event an unnatural condition, even for reef fish, which more often than not frequent the backwaters or eddies and not the main currents running between or alongside reefs. Even if strong aeration is required, this should be diffused through several airstones. For a 3-foot tank we normally use two such stones.

Aerator pumps should be located in an area free from heavy tobacco smoke, paint or chemical fumes, exhaust gases from cars, etc.

Siting of Tank. The tank is best located in a draught-free position away from radiators or air conditioners, and preferably where it will receive several hours of natural sunlight per day. We have covered the points relating to natural light in more detail in the lighting section.

Seasoning and Preparation. All tanks need seasoning before use, particularly those with a cement content. For these we recommend at least fourteen days' seasoning and soaking in several changes of water. The last of these should be seawater, followed by a final rinsing out with freshwater. Care must be taken not to fill tanks too quickly particularly when they are new, because they need plenty of time to adapt to the stress.

3. Tank Arrangement

Basic requirements

Tank arrangement is very much a question of personal taste and will depend largely upon the types of specimens which you wish to display. Any arrangement should have as its foundation dead coral rock which has *not* been chemically treated nor artificially coloured. There is no point in using choice (though dead) coral specimens for this – the idea is only to take care of the *pH* factor and to provide a base upon which to place the living inhabitants. The coral which we use is old coral rock fresh from the sea – honeycombed with many holes and suitable as a planting-place for sponge fragments and a lodging for tube worms. It is usually grey in colour and craggy in appearance.

Coral rock which has been collected locally in the tropics must be placed in aerated water as soon as possible after it is picked up because it will inevitably house a large, unseen, living population. If you are setting up a tank in a temperate climate you will have to use long dead coral and make sure that it is properly (but not chemically) sterilized. Once such coral has been in a natural aquarium for any length of time, however, it will have acquired a population of its own and must thereafter be treated just as you would treat any coral rock picked up recently on the beach.

Fish and other creatures will need deep cover at times both for security and as a protection from prolonged artificial lighting. The reefs themselves provide natural refuges into which the coral fishes can escape to safety in split seconds. If they have similar conditions in the tank they will not be afraid to flaunt themselves in their full brilliance.

Although a reef cannot be simulated exactly the overall effect should be true. As a general rule, we aim to create an underground network of caves and tunnels. If coral rock is scarce and a steeply rising layout is desired, use large broken plant-pots to form the interior. These give a magnificent inter-connecting cave system. Deck this with dead coral rock or old clam shells. Once such an arrangement is set up and furnished with

36

corals you will find your fishes coming through the 'reef' from a number of directions, wriggling through apparently impossibly small gaps, just as in the wild. The bottom photograph facing page 33 shows a small fish on the point of leaving one such cave. The fish is thought to have been a green wrasse. Members of this family seem to need rocks and caves almost as much as they need sand. For the sake of such fishes it is desirable to have at least some caves giving direct access to the sand at the bottom of the tank so that the cave has a sandy floor. An example is shown in the bottom photograph facing page 49. There is a problem here, though, in that the creamy anemone has moved rather too close to the mouth of the cave.

This raises the question of a layout suitable for invertebrates. Large upturned clam shells make a good resting-place for anemones. These creatures, if happily settled, rarely wander and every effort should be made to place them satisfactorily before introducing the main coral display. A wandering anemone is very troublesome and can smother some specimens and spoil others with its nematocysts. They should be placed where they will block neither entrances to caves nor routes favoured by the fishes.

Tube worms can be inserted into crannies to display their magnificent plumes to advantage. A convenient method is to train a clump of these on one piece of honeycombed coral. Make sure that they are securely placed so that they cannot be knocked down. When dislodged and lying on the rock or sand they are particularly vulnerable to nibbling by small crabs.

The only corals which can safely be placed on sand are: *Fungia* (all species), *Herpolitha limax, Oulastrea crispata, Polyphyllia talpina* and *Trachyphyllia geoffroyi*. Such corals can be placed on the sand with confidence. Others would have their living polyps smothered and stinking black sand would result. (Black sand and the offending coral must always be removed as soon as discovered; sometimes the coral can be saved by cleaning away the dead part.)

Any living coral which has a large dead coral base may be placed upon sand provided that only the dead part touches the sand.

Corals which cannot be placed on a sand base can have a sand background if you put them on a piece of dead rock standing in the sand and sweep the sand around the base to complete the illusion. Be careful, however, that this is not too close to a cave occupied by a pistol prawn – these creatures can excavate huge piles of sand and may well silt up corals in their neighbourhood. A wrasse going to bed under the sand can

37

also do the same thing, but in this case all that is needed is to rinse the coral clear in the morning by waving it about in the tank. Then move it to a safer place. In the early stages, until you have gained experience, we recommend that you limit the sand to one part of the tank and set a firm barrier of low rocks to keep it in place.

Plenty of sand is a necessity if you wish to keep sea olives and other sand dwellers and a 2-inch layer is recommended in such cases. These animals should have the longest possible stretch of sand, preferably the whole front length of the tank. Wrasses will also appreciate this. Sand adds to the general brightness of the display and gives a sunlit look. As an alternative, we have sometimes used coral pebbles which are also attractive, especially if used for only part of the tank. An all-pebble bottom can have rather a cold, grey look. Fine shingle and even fine sand may be used – although mulm-type residues become rather too conspicuous if the sand is very fine.

Corals must not be put too close to each other as the nematocysts will kill neighbouring polyps. Nor should they be put where they will be cut off from the main source of light. In such a position they will grow pale, eject their zooxanthellae and finally die.

Tubastrea aurea and *T. diaphana,* having no zooxanthellae, are notable exceptions to this rule and normally favour shaded places on the reef. We find, however, that even these corals do better if they get some light. The bright-orange or lemon colour of *T. aurea* can liven up dull corners and if fed with fresh plankton or newly hatched brine shrimp it will flourish indefinitely, even breeding. You must make sure, however, that you do not import its enemy, a small papillated nudibranch of the same colour which feeds upon this coral. It is difficult to detect when very young, but soon grows and becomes progressively more hungry. There does not seem to be any alternative food on which it can be fed, which is a pity because it is a very pretty creature.

If instead of having a community tank you wish to try to breed clowns then live corals should be kept to a minimum. Breeding tanks should contain a good proportion of coral rock to take care of the *pH* factor and they should have as much encrusting algae as possible. Sand can be used to assist the overall balance.

An interesting variation is to have a tank set up with sand and coral rock and a display of *Cerianthus*. Although extremely beautiful these creatures are very dangerous to small fishes and will damage every living coral which their tentacles happen to touch. Tube worms, hermit crabs, sea olives, starfish, clams and perhaps some large fishes could also be

38

kept with them, but you may think that a rather stark arrangement better emphasizes the beauty of the *Cerianthus*. Sea urchins make an excellent foil for them, though as a general principle we do not recommend the use of these. If the supply of sand is short, *Cerianthus* will thrive when planted (literally) in a flower-pot filled with sand which can be sunk into a surround of pebbles or rock. In such a case you could not, of course, keep other sand dwellers in the same tank and would need a separate flower-pot for each *Cerianthus*.

Setting up the tank

The tank should be seasoned as described elsewhere, particularly if a lot of concrete has been used in its construction.

For the first stage only water, sand, coral rocks and 'reef' building materials are essential. Once the tank is completely ready, tested and seasoned, the next steps vary according to whether you are using 'live' sand (i.e. sand which has been freshly collected and kept in aerated water to preserve the minute life within it) or sterile 'washed' sand. In the former case it is immaterial whether the water is put in before or after the coral rock foundation. We normally start by putting in the rock because this seems to be easier. It may be arranged in any manner you like, bearing in mind the creatures which you will want to keep and the need to provide caves and escape routes. This foundation must be very firmly constructed so that it can neither rock nor topple. After this the tank can be filled with water and then the 'live' sand may be tipped quickly into the desired area. It can be distributed by hand in difficult corners. Do not worry about clouding the water, it will clear within twenty-four hours unless you have a large mud content. Fan the sand away from rocks and shells, particularly those on which you plan to place anemones. The tank should then be left for one or two days for the water and the sand to settle. Keep it aerated the whole time.

Sterile sand, i.e. that which has been washed in freshwater and then dried, needs a different treatment. In this case the rock and the sand should be placed in the tank before decanting the water. Paper, preferably plain strong tissue paper, should then be placed carefully over the whole area and the water poured in as gently as possible. Even so, cloudiness may persist for a considerable time. The paper should be removed when the water has been poured in: its purpose is only to act as a 'blanket' during this operation.

If freshly collected sand has been used the water should become crystal clear within twenty-four to forty-eight hours. If it is not clear, look for trouble amongst the rocks in the form of undiscovered sponge. Our advice is to quarantine the rock and sand together in the tank for at least a week before adding your main display – this may save considerable time and trouble later.

Provided that the water has cleared satisfactorily at the end of this period – now is the time to plant the anemones in the desired locations. Do not do this before decanting the sand or they will inevitably be covered with a scattering of grains which may irritate them and start a fit of wandering.

Float the anemones down to the desired place; a little handling may help them to settle, but this must be gentle. If the first planting is unsuccessful repeat the process very gently. Should the creature remain with its pedal disc uppermost and still show no inclination to settle, it is sometimes effective to place it in position and then press gently but firmly on the pedal disc to help it take hold. In the event of persistent failure the best course is to return the anemone to the quarantine tank and try again another day. We do feel that it is important to settle these creatures before introducing coral.

At the anemone settling stage, tube worms, tunicates, crabs, prawns and similar creatures can be put into position as these are unlikely to be worried even if the anemones refuse to behave. Sponge can also be put in at the same time. Ideally, the sponge should already be growing on its own piece of rock. If not, unattached sponges or fragments can be planted in small holes in the rocks in the front of the tank. If they turn grey, yellow or brown, remove them immediately. When only a small part is affected this can be broken off and the balance replanted.

Now the tank is ready to be furnished with corals, fishes and any remaining creatures.

Some suitable tank populations are suggested at the end of this chapter. These inventories are only intended as a guide which need not be followed too closely. Our selections are based upon hardiness, size, colour and general compatibility of the creatures. If you wish to make your own choice of corals, fishes and other creatures from those described in this book you will need to take heed of the warnings given in the sections concerned regarding incompatibility of certain fishes with certain corals, tube worms, etc.

So far as fishes are concerned, the old freshwater rule of 1 inch of fish to 1 gallon of water may comfortably be exceeded and we have had successful tanks containing double this incidence. For safety, however, the rule is a wise one and sea fishes generally seem to be more aggressive than their freshwater counterparts. You will certainly have far less trouble with injuries from fighting where the fishes have ample swimming room and enough space to establish their own little domains if they wish. Besides, disease strikes more readily and more disastrously at a crowded tank. As with coral, err towards underpopulation rather than over-population. Higher densities are possible but are not essential to a well-planned tank.

If butterfly fish have to be avoided because of the risk to tube worms, then we recommend Malayan angel fish as suitable and very hardy substitutes.

We have not listed sea mushrooms in any of our inventories because they are difficult to find, but if available they should be included because they do well and even thrive in temperate climates.

Suggested inventory for tank 3 feet × 2-foot 6-inches × 2 feet. Such a tank lends itself to the building of a central massif with plenty of inter-communicating caves and four tunnels, one leading to each side of the tank. Several inches must be left between the topmost specimens and the glass so that algal deposits can be removed.

CORALS

Size	Qty	Description	Comments
4–8 inches	1	*Platygyra lamellina*	Hardiest and best known of the 'brain' corals. Must not be over-shadowed. We recommend a central position under the light or maximum access to any day-light.
6 inches	1	*Euphyllia fimbriata*	We keep specimens up to 18 inches, often as centrepieces and they make a very effective display.
4–6 inches	3 or 4	*Goniopora* (any species)	Too much of this coral gives a monotonous effect but it is most attractive if used in moderation. *Alveopora excelsa* may be substituted as it has much the same appearance except that the polyps are shorter.
4–6 inches	1	*Symphyllia nobilis* or *Lobophyllia hemprichii*	These have larger proportions and bolder patterns than *Platygyra lamellina* and can be very striking. Light is important to them but they do not fade quite so readily.

41

Size	Qty	Description	Comments
3–6 inches	1 or 2	*Pectinia lactuca*	Although this coral is brittle, it is relatively hardy and has beautiful flowerlike shapes.
3–6 inches	1	*Turbinaria peltata*	Given good light this is hardy although inclined to have resting periods. It is a very robust looking coral and provides an excellent foil for the more delicate specimens.
3–4 inches	1	*Euphyllia glabrescens*	Leave plenty of room for the tentacles to expand.
3–4 inches	1	*Trachyphyllia geoffroyi*	There is a wonderful range of colours.
2–3 inches	2 or 3	*Fungia* (any species)	Perhaps 1 *F. actiniformis* on the sand and 1 or 2 *F. fungites* on the rocks.
1–2 inches	3 or 4	*Tubastrea aurea*	These golden, lemon- or orange-coloured corals brighten dull patches and do not need much light. Never place on sand.
1–2 inches	1 or 2	*Tubastrea diaphana*	Less hardy than *T. aurea* but its dark almost bronze colour is the perfect foil for that coral. When dying does not foul the tank.

FISHES

Size	Qty	Description	Comments
3 inches	1	cowfish	If you can get a small specimen it will add character to the tank.
3 inches	2 or 3	butterfly fish	Introduce these all at once and watch for bullying – if this occurs remove victim.
3 inches	2 or 3	wrasses	Choose the smaller species and give them plenty of sand.
2–3 inches	2 prs or 3 prs	clown fish	Use only 1 pair if you have a large species such as *A. ephippium*.
2–3 inches	4 to 6	dascyllus	
2–3 inches	4 to 6	demoiselles	Watch these lest they fight.
2–3 inches	2 to 4	gobies or blennies	

If you wish to keep tube worms you should perhaps omit butterfly fish as they will occasionally peck at them. Or you could reduce the risk, and the damage, by trying only one of these fish.

OTHER CREATURES

Size	Qty	Description	Comments
4–6 inches	1 per clown	anemones mixed colours	To provide homes for clowns and to add colour. If different species of clowns are introduced we advise placing the anemones in clumps of two with the width of the tank between them. This will avoid undue fighting between the different species.
Various	1 or more	starfish	For colour and a touch of the exotic. *Linckia* – the blue star – if available does well in a large tank.
	6–12	cowries	Choose the smaller types not exceeding about 1 inch in length and mix the species so as to get an attractive variety of shells. Cowries will eat dying coral polyps and are therefore most useful.
	2–6	common tube worms	Either use in a clump or dotted in rock or coral crevices – place reasonably near to each other to assist breeding.
	–	bottle-brush tube worms	These have bright colours and are most fascinating. They normally live in *Porites* coral and the number which you can accommodate depends not upon the small worms themselves but upon the size of the piece of rock in which they are growing.

Many small creatures can also be added, such as mantis shrimps, sea squirts, tunicates and small univalves and bivalves. We do not advise using *Tridacna* clams until you have had reasonable experience of the system as a whole. Much the same applies to sponges – small pieces can be placed where they are easily observed and removed if necessary, but do not be too ambitious. A few plants can also be added. Members of the *Caulerpa* genus are among the more reliable, but even these need watching.

Suggested inventory for tank 36 inches × 15 inches × 18 inches As this tank would be too narrow for a central foundation of rock, the coral will have to be banked up at the back. We suggest the following specimens:

CORALS

Size	Qty	Description	Comments
4–5 inches	1	*Euphyllia fimbriata*	You could use 1 or 2 of the smaller *E. glabrescens* instead.
4–5 inches	1	*Turbinaria peltata*	
3–4 inches	2	*Goniopora* (any species)	
3–4 inches	1	*Pectinia lactuca*	
3–4 inches	1	*Platygyra lamellina*	Or *Symphyllia nobilis* or *Lobophyllia hemprichii.*
3–4 inches	2	*Trachyphyllia geoffroyi*	
2–3 inches	1 or 2	*Fungia* (any species)	
1–2 inches	several	*Tubastrea aurea* and *T. diaphana*	
1–2 inches	1	*Oulastrea crispata*	

FISHES

Size	Qty	Description	Comments
3 inches	1	butterfly fish	
3 inches	2	wrasses (small ones)	
2–3 inches	1 pr	clown fish	As with the wrasses, try to get small species.
2–3 inches	2	dascyllus	
2–3 inches	2	demoiselles	
2–3 inches	2	gobies or blennies	Try to get 1 male and 1 female.

OTHER CREATURES

Size	Qty	Description	Comments
4–6 inches	2	anemones	Try to get one white and one pink. If your clowns are a pair, place the anemones close together.
Various	1	starfish	You can use one typical five-armed starfish with the rigid body or several of the small brittle stars which are so fascinating to watch at feeding time.
1 inch	6	cowries	Choose a selection of the smaller species.
Various	3	common tube worms	

As in the case of the larger tank, many other creatures can be added, but keep to the smaller sizes.

4. Tank Maintenance and Feeding

One of the great advantages of the natural system is that water *need* not be changed for many years. In practice, however, we find that partial water changes made periodically will help to keep the tanks looking attractive. There is also the inevitable routine work to be done to clear unsightly algae growing over the glass.

Salinity is another factor which has to be carefully watched, particularly if the glass covering the tank lights is close to the aeration stones.

Due to the large proportion of naturally calcareous rock the problem of change in *pH* is not present.

Uneaten food rarely presents any trouble as unseen scavengers such as bristle worms will see to this and will prevent undue increase in the more harmful forms of bacteria caused by decaying food.

Water. Although plants and some soft corals and the sea mushrooms will thrive for long periods without any water change, we believe that for full tank health partial changes of water should be made every three months. This is particularly advisable for aquarists in temperate climates where corals will inevitably be costly. The water-changing operation should be combined with the siphoning off of mulm and mud deposits from crevices and caves. Some life will inevitably be lost during such operations and to minimize this danger we advise filtering the water through a fine-meshed net so as to rescue any small crabs or shrimps drawn through the tube. The replacement water should restore the tank 'balance' and possibly add new supplies of phytoplankton. Our view is that the appearance of the tanks – particularly community tanks – is improved by periodical siphoning off of mulm, etc., and replacement of the water drawn off. If it is wished to breed fishes – clowns and demoiselles in particular – the water should be changed as infrequently as possible. But even in this case, if a mated pair consistently refuses to start spawning behaviour it may be worth while to try changing an inch or so of water as there is some evidence that this may stimulate them.

Evaporation of seawater should be made good with tap-water to correct salinity. If the light-cover glass is close to the surface of the water and spray from the aeration stone can fall back on to this glass it will accumulate heavy deposits of evaporated salt. Over a period this will form a thick crust which not only reduces the light but can also cause a drop in salinity. It is therefore advisable to wipe the glass clean once a week and redissolve the accumulated salts in the water. If this task is left too long, dark green algae will form amongst the salts which cannot then be redissolved in the water without turning it an unsightly green. A hydrometer is a useful piece of equipment particularly for the inland aquarist.

Algae and mulm. Tanks exposed to a reasonable amount of sunlight will develop heavy and unsightly accumulations of algae over the glass surfaces. These can easily be scraped off with a razor blade and the cleared algae will settle on the bottom thence to be siphoned from the tank together with any mulm. As mentioned earlier, this operation should be performed through a fine-meshed net as many types of small animals find shelter amongst deposits of mulm.

So far as deposits of algae on the back glass are concerned, we never clean these in our main tanks, preferring to encourage this growth which provides a useful feeding ground for cowries and other primarily vegetarian creatures. We also think that the mass of algae helps towards a balance and increases the daylight oxygen-generating capacity of the tank.

Sand, rocks and coral. Sand can become unsightly in the course of time and algae will even grow in the top surfaces. We periodically draw off the top surface of sand when siphoning out deposits of mulm and replace it with fresh sand. No doubt the sea olives appreciate a change occasionally and so do those fishes, such as wrasses, which like to suck or chew the sand.

Rocks, corals and other main items of tank furniture are best left alone unless you are in the process of a major tank change.

Major tank changes for purposes of reconstruction and rehabilitation. As in freshwater tanks, an amazing amount of dirt accumulates within the various crevices in the rock. When performing a major tank change we draw off the old water into pails and use these to hold the corals and rocks during tank cleaning operations. (The various creatures will survive without aeration for this time, but if it is available an aerator should be used.) Just before replacing the corals and rocks in their tank we give them a thorough rinsing through in this 'old' seawater, which is not itself used again. We feel that when setting up a refurbished tank it is preferable to use completely new seawater. The creatures will in any event have received a severe shock and replacement in completely new water will assist them to resettle in the shortest possible time.

We sometimes economize by very thoroughly rinsing the old sand, small quantities at a time, in a fine-meshed net in the 'old' seawater and then reuse this sand to deck the tank, but if new sand is readily available it is better and quicker to use it.

During such tank changes plants and algae should be handled as gently as possible and lightly rinsed in the old seawater to remove any mulm. Rocks on which the green silky algae are growing should similarly be washed and then replaced in positions where they will obtain the maximum amount of light.

This is a good time to inspect the bases of your coral although it is unlikely that, after so long, any undesirable deposits of wild sponge will be present. Nevertheless, some of the crevices may hold decomposing matter which has escaped notice by normal tank scavengers.

If the base of the tank is of concrete this should also be checked carefully to ensure that no rust is seeping through from the metal reinforcement.

Daily maintenance. Daily maintenance is negligible as unless one has been extraordinarily lavish there should be no uneaten food particles and maintenance is confined to scrutinizing the fishes for any signs of disease, checking that anemones have not wandered and smothered corals and that the corals are free from sand and receiving their full share of light.

Feeding. Corals, sponges, sea squirts, etc., are mostly fed by self-generating supplies of plankton. Within the confined conditions of a tank, however, this supply may not be sufficient to keep a heavily populated tank in good health for long periods. The natural zooplankton content should therefore be supplemented once or twice a week by feeds of newly hatched brine shrimp. We think that this is particularly important for aquarists in temperate climates.

Most marine fishes are naturally carnivorous and will also welcome a supply of small live shrimps. A number of people regularly use guppies for feeding and these appear to be readily accepted by most fishes and by anemones. Some of the larger clowns will cope with surprisingly large shrimps but the process is rather cruel, involving the tearing of the shrimp to pieces, and we do not feed them live shrimps unless they have been without live food for a long period. Out here the main standby is dead uncooked shrimp or prawn which we have chopped very finely and scattered broadcast throughout the tank.

We feed close to anemones so that most of the uneaten particles which escape the fishes are automatically retrieved. Unless the anemones are in a difficult position we rarely feed them deliberately as they inevitably collect this surplus food. Should you wish to feed anemones or *Cerianthus* individually do not place the food into the stomach directly as their feeding system depends on the food being first seized by the tentacles and then transferred to the stomach. This presumably releases the necessary digestive enzymes.

Some of the corals with longer polyps such as *Fungia* and *Euphyllia* also appear to absorb small pieces of this meat. *Tubastrea aurea* will bloom if a piece of shrimp is placed near to it and we normally squeeze the fragment above the *T. aurea* to give it some juice. A certain amount of this juice may also be beneficial to lower forms of life provided that it is not used excessively.

You should leave some pieces of food lying around either on the sand or the rocks for the night eaters, shyer fishes and various scavengers such as crabs, bristle worms, etc. If you have sea olives in the sand they will readily surface and absorb any uneaten particles of shrimp. Do not leave such particles directly against the glass – this makes it difficult for some creatures to reach them without frightening themselves by coming into contact with the glass. Cowfish, for example, cannot reach food placed against the glass however hard they try to manœuvre themselves into position, because of the projecting 'horns'.

If you have herbivorous creatures such as *Lambis lambis* it is necessary to ensure that adequate supplies of algae are available. For such animals we cultivate the fine green alga which we call 'blanket weed' and feed them with it several times a week. Sometimes we put into the tank a stone with another fine silky green alga growing on it – this looks rather like grass and if removed after 'cropping' by the *Lambis lambis* and placed in a tank out of doors the alga will usually re-grow.

A number of fishes such as rabbit fish and scats and creatures like nudibranchs also welcome this soft green food and it is a good idea when cultivating 'blanket weed' to sow brine shrimp eggs in the same tank.

We have not had reason to experiment with the use of white worms or grindal worm for feeding corals or anemones. These have, however, been

8. Grey hooded wrasse. In the left foreground a brain coral *(Platygyra lamellina)* and at right a *Trachyphyllia geoffroyi* which has been damaged by the *Cerianthus* tentacles

9. General view of a tank. The fish in the foreground is *Abudefduf oxydon*
   Photograph by the author

10. Butterfly fish *(Chelmon rostratus)* and wrasses. In foreground a *Fungia* coral. A *Radianthus* anemone is in left background and tentacles of *Cerianthus* show at the right margin

11. *Coris gaimard* with starfish and golden wrasse. The coral in foreground is *Fungia fungites*
Photograph by the author

used by a very experienced aquarist friend in the U.K. with most satis-factory results and we have no doubt that they will be of great benefit to the inland aquarist, particularly in temperate climates.

Dry food is valueless so far as invertebrates are concerned, but we find that most fishes will in due course come to accept it quite readily and appear to thrive on this diet. They should not, of course, be kept solely on dried food.

We do not think that daphnia or similar creatures used for freshwater fishes will be suitable for tropical marines. The breeding of mosquitoes is (understandably) illegal in Singapore, but in Djakarta their larvae are sold by itinerant fish vendors and we find that our fishes there devour them avidly. Even fastidious eaters such as species of *Apogon* love it, and so do anemones. Mosquito larvae approximates to the larger forms of zooplankton found in the sea, and should prove invaluable as a natural food for marine fishes. A food used for freshwater fishes which we mis-trust is tubefix worm. Although some marines appear to welcome it, we had a bad outbreak of disease after using tubefix and felt that it could possibly have been the carrier. Finely shredded garden worms are used by some aquarists and the fishes are reported to accept these readily. As in the case of most living creatures, diet should be varied so far as possible – although fishes can survive on a relatively monotonous diet they respond better to variety.

Feeding of fry. It is essential that suitable food should virtually swim into the mouths of the newly hatched fry. In the case of freshwater fishes, this food is provided by infusoria and can be fed in relatively heavy quantities. We doubt whether the normal freshwater infusoria would be the right type of food for marine fry, but feel that it is well while experi-menting with cultures using seawater instead of freshwater and perhaps with some of the proprietary products. In view of the different circum-stances it would be advisable to aerate such cultures during the breeding process.

Aquarists in the tropics with ready access to the sea and sufficient time can try towing for plankton with a fine net: this food must then be fed as quickly as possible to the baby fishes. Once they are free-swimming they should be at the stage where brine shrimp will be sufficient and after that they can have micro worms. Mosquito larvae are not suitable for very young fishes and should not be allowed in the tank with them.

This problem of food for young marine fry is still not solved. Dr Fishelson comments in his papers that his young *Dascyllus aruanas* fed on minute copepods in the water. This was clearly proved as the food could be seen in the stomachs of the fry. He also fed them boiled egg yolk. Despite this, all died unaccountably on the fifth day although immediately previously they had appeared to be in good health and feeding well. It is possible that fry also require additional trace elements, phytoplankton and vegetable matter, as well as minute zooplankton.

5. The Health of the Aquarium

In 'natural' system tanks we are concerned with the health of a large number of animals of which the fishes represent only a small proportion. The main health hazards are:

Extremes of heat and cold, or sudden changes in temperature,
Unfavourable chemical conditions such as metal, cement or putty poisoning,
Insufficient light, which mainly affects invertebrates,
Lack of oxygen,
Improper feeding,
Overcrowding and/or inclusion of unsuitable or incompatible specimens,
Poor hygiene,
Fish diseases.

The first six of the above hazards can be avoided by attention to the advice which we have given in other parts of this book.

Hygiene

Poor hygiene is the most usual cause of trouble. Thorough quarantining of anything destined for the tank, including sand and rock, is essential. (Whether or not you quarantine water must depend upon whether you consider that too much of the plankton will die before the quarantine period is up. We do not ourselves quarantine water but prefer to give the fishes the benefit of really fresh seawater.) Sand and rock – water, too, if you decide to quarantine it – should, like the fishes and invertebrates, be kept in aerated tanks whilst in quarantine. The quarantine period is ten to fourteen days and starts from the date of introduction of the last specimen into the quarantine tank. This precaution applies whether you are collecting your own specimens or buying them from a dealer. If you are continually collecting your own specimens, you will need to quarantine them in batches and should have a number of tanks for this purpose.

If any fish in a batch becomes sick, it must be removed and treated separately; the rest of the batch must then be quarantined afresh after any necessary precautionary treatment. In the case of clown fishes, which are notoriously prone to *Oodinium,* it may be worth while treating them with the copper sulphate solution recommended as a prophylactic immediately on receipt, even if no symptoms are then observed. This is discussed in more detail in the section on *Oodinium.*

Invertebrates will succumb to most, if not all, of the cures for fish diseases. Fishes requiring treatment, preventive or otherwise, should therefore be removed to a separate tank, even though this means depriving the clowns of anemones for a while.

Quarantine tanks should be kept well away from main tanks: ideally they should be in a different room. Similarly strict segregation should be observed with quarantine equipment, i.e. nets, cleaning rags, dippers, etc. These should be reserved exclusively for the use of the particular tank concerned. Synthetic sponges or sponge cloths are best for cleaning and these should be sterilized frequently by boiling. Nets should also be sterilized regularly. No disinfectants, insecticides, paint sprays, soaps or detergents should be used in the vicinity of the tanks and preferably not even in the same room except under supervision. If the floor has to be swept, the tank covers must be kept closed during this work to prevent dust and fluff from getting into the water.

Hands which are liable to be dipped into fish tanks should be free of soap, lotions, etc. After dipping into one tank they should be thoroughly rinsed in fresh running water before touching another.

Do not move specimens indiscriminately from one tank to another unless you are absolutely sure that the donor tank is free from disease. We suspect that one of our outbreaks of *Oodinium* was spread by the transfer of small pieces of coral rock from a tank in which an incipient outbreak had not yet been detected. Presumably the coral rock was harbouring resting parasites.

Newly established tanks need daily inspection. Fishes should be scrutinized for signs of disease, particularly *Oodinium.* Keep a careful watch for dying sponge, coral, anemones and clams. Sponge is an excellent barometer of tank health once it is fully established as it is usually the first creature to die in any general poisoning. Newly planted sponge is a different matter and is very unpredictable.

Obviously sick fishes, or even those suspected of sickness, should be isolated and any dead bodies removed. This latter precaution is contrary to the principals of the 'natural' system which would leave the bacteria to demolish such rotting protein, but apart from the aesthetic viewpoint, we dislike leaving a body because it may spread disease. If the fishes die behind rocks or you lose an obviously ageing fish, it is a different matter, but the question 'Did it die of an infectious disease?' is always one which you should ask yourself before deciding whether or not to hunt for the corpse.

Should you have any case of an infectious fish disease, all the fishes in the same tank must be given precautionary treatment, even those not obviously affected. This is particularly important in the case of *Oodinium* and is the general rule. An exception to the rule is wasting disease which seems to affect only clowns and no precautions appear to be necessary in the case of other fishes. All clowns, however, albeit seemingly unaffected, should be isolated if any one in a tank is stricken with this sickness. Isolation may save some which have not yet contracted the disease. In the case of a single attack of fungus affecting only one fish, no precautions are likely to be necessary to protect others in the same tank.

Before dealing with specific fish diseases, we will describe disasters which are likely to affect the whole tank. The death of any large invertebrate may do this, but it is important to remember that, for example, a piece of dying sponge or an anemone which is sick may be *both a symptom and a further cause of poisoning*.

General tank poisoning

The water of an established tank should be crystal clear although in some cases it may have a very faint amber tint. When the water becomes a strong amber, or takes on a milky opaque look and has an oily appearance, then there is something wrong. This appearance is usually coupled with an unpleasant smell and the fishes more often than not will show signs of distress. Do not, however, confuse this condition with the greyish or brownish murk emitted by breeding tube worms or with the cloudiness caused by the breeding of large corals such as *Euphyllia fimbriata*. The cloudiness of tube worm breeding will clear completely within twenty-four hours and that of the corals within a much shorter period. There will be no smell in either instance, the fishes and corals will be blooming and obviously happy with the unexpected increase in plankton. The breeding coral itself, however, particularly if it be *E.*

53

fimbriata may appear disconcerting. The tentacles will be grotesquely shortened and the body bloated, with a widely gaping 'mouth'. A short period of observation will be certain to reveal the true state of affairs.

Strong smell associated with dark, amberish water, within twenty-four hours of setting up a quarantine tank usually indicates a very high degree of contamination from a number of sources due to indiscriminate collection. No amount of water changing will help and the complete collection should be returned to the sea as quickly as possible.

If, however, there is obvious distress, smell or murk not associated with breeding or a recent unquarantined collection, then look around for trouble due to one or more of the following causes:

(a) Sick or dying anemones or clams. In this condition an anemone will be shunned by any attendant clowns, the stomach will almost certainly be extended, the tentacles flabby and it will probably have become detached from its resting-place. Slime may sometimes be extruded.

The anemone should be removed immediately to a plastic bucket of fresh seawater. Strong aeration may revive it, but this is not likely. In this state a large anemone can rapidly poison even a well-established tank.

The most likely cause of anemones' sickness is metal poisoning, to which they are particularly susceptible. A friend in England had some which flourished for more than a year when he suddenly began to lose them rapidly. Investigation showed that he had recently made good evaporation in their tank with freshwater and there had been some lead in the container used for collecting this. An immediate change of water prevented further casualties.

Clams and anemones will also die if they have insufficient light, but in this case, you should notice them gradually failing.

Large dying clams of 4–6 inches or more can cause severe poisoning, but they usually give forewarning by becoming progressively paler and the gape gets steadily wider. These creatures require strong light for full health. The glorious iridescent sheen of the mantle is derived from a vast population of zooxanthellae, minute single-celled plants, that live within the flesh. The clam cultures and feeds on these plants. Poor light will naturally reduce the plant population drastically and the clam will in effect die of starvation. Remove any sick clam to a separate bucket of aerated seawater and give strong light, preferably sunlight. For safety, we do not recommend the use of clams of above 2–3 inches in size until you have become very experienced in the care of these creatures.

54

(b) Sick or dying corals. These are usually obvious. On corals such as *Goniopora* the surface becomes covered with a greyish black or whitish film rather like a mould. Remove the coral from the tank as gently as possible to prevent the decomposing matter from dispersing into the water. Thoroughly rinse the coral in a bucket of seawater and replace it. In most cases this will be sufficient. If you are unsure about it, quarantine the coral for a few days or put it in the front of the tank where you can watch it. Some corals can be treated by cutting or chipping off the piece affected, but such action should be avoided if possible.

Corals dying from lack of light become progressively paler as they eject their zooxanthellae. They will not pollute the tank and will merely wilt away. If removed in time, i.e. before tissue wastage commences, and placed in better light (sunlight if at all possible) they will regain their normal colour within about six weeks. This will also apply to smaller anemones such as sea mushrooms, which can also become almost white from lack of light.

Corals which have died from being smothered in sand will be found to have left an area of blackened sand around and beneath them. After removal of the coral, siphon off the black sand through a large-bore tube. You may well be surprised at the extent to which this deposit has spread under other healthy-looking sand. Make sure that all traces are removed. After removing the black sand and dead coral, a partial change of water will be sufficient to restore the tank.

(c) Dying sponge. This is most likely to be hidden within cavities in the coral or at the base of clumps of zoanthids. The condition is mostly found in newly collected specimens and will never be present in those purchased from a dealer in Europe or North America. A bad smell is a reliable pointer to this type of trouble, especially if there are no other obvious causes for the odour.

In such a case, the best course is to remove all coral and rock and to sniff each piece individually. The offending piece or pieces will readily be found. The only cure is immediate removal from the tank. It may be possible to remove the rotten sponge and to return the rock or coral to the tank. We do not advise this, however, as in some cases sponge grows right through the rock and there may well be other cavities containing large pieces of dying sponge. The best remedy is to place the affected rock in a separate tank until you are sure the trouble has been cured. A complete or partial change of the water in the original tank may be required depending upon the extent of the original contamination.

When specimen pieces of sponge, properly rooted and established, start to die off this may be due to natural causes or to starvation. It may be possible to save the unaffected parts of the sponge by nipping off the discoloured portions and re-planting the others. In such cases metal, cement, or putty poisoning should also be suspected.

(d) Metal, cement or putty poisoning. Metal poisoning is difficult to detect unless there are obvious signs of rust or other corrosion and where this is suspected, the only course is to investigate all possible sources of drip-back from metal surfaces into the tank, such as screws, hinges, light fittings, etc., and to examine all the metal or metal-reinforced parts, including the floor of the tank beneath the sand. The problem with this type of poisoning is that it is likely to develop gradually after the tank has been in use for some time.

Cement or putty poisoning is most likely to be found at the tank edges where cement or putty has been used to secure the glass. Look for traces of black sand spreading outwards from the glass or alongside it. In some cases, a white or light grey film will be found along the glass running above the surface of the sand. The blackness is probably due to lack of oxygen at lower levels permitting anaerobic bacteria to flourish. In this case the only remedy is to empty the tank and to reglaze it with a more suitable medium. The black sand must not, of course, be reused.

Checklist

If the tank does not settle down and you get persistent losses of fishes and other specimens without obvious signs of disease, we recommend that you run through the following list:

Is there:
Sufficient light;
Sufficient space;
Sufficient aeration;
Any crowding of corals against each other;
A *Cerianthus* whose tentacles could touch a nearby coral or other invertebrates – they can stretch enormously after dark;
An anemone which has moved and has settled on top of a coral or other creature;
The possibility that the tentacles of such a wandering anemone may be touching adjacent corals or invertebrates;
Corals silted up by sand, or any non-sand coral placed on sand;

Sick or dying anemones or clams;

Dying sponge – visible or invisible. If your rocks or corals are collected by yourself, do not forget that sponge can tunnel through and form immense pockets behind seemingly healthy living rock. In many cases such dying concealed sponge turns the surrounding rock black assisting location of the trouble;

Any sepia extruding creature such as an octopus;

A red feather star giving off dye;

The possibility of metal, cement or putty poisoning;

Danger from draughts or excessive local heating;

Possible contamination from disinfectants, insecticides, paints or fumes;

Poisoning due to detergents, soap or hand lotions;

Anything which has been dropped into the tank, perhaps by children;

Any marked change in salinity (anemones are particularly susceptible to trouble from this cause which means that care must be taken when topping up the tank with freshwater – frequent small toppings up to replace evaporation are best);

Any evidence of excessively heavy feeding or anything wrong with the food supply?

When you think that you have found the cause of the trouble, double check to ensure that it is not merely ONE of many small faults.

Treatment of fish diseases

The following general notes apply to the treatment of all fish diseases and injuries.

Do not dab at or touch eyes or gills and try to keep the fishes' heads and gills under the water whilst working quickly to avoid increasing shock.

Use sterile seawater for making up stock mixtures and for filling the treatment tanks. Sterile seawater can be obtained by keeping one or two plastic containers in a dark place without aeration for a fortnight, after which most of the plankton content will be dead. The water should then be filtered into other containers so that it is ready for use at any time. Natural unfiltered seawater fresh from the sea may be used in an emergency but the drawback is that you may thereby risk introducing infection to already weakened fishes. A further disadvantage of using fresh seawater is that chemicals such as copper sulphate or methylene blue kill the zooplankton leaving the water with an unpleasant smell – this does not appear to impede recovery of the fish but is best avoided. Another expedient is to siphon off a certain amount of water from other tanks (which will also, however, contain some zooplankton). Artificial sea-water can be used and will form adequate sterile water at short notice. This will naturally create reconversion problems after the cure when the fishes are at their weakest, but in a real emergency such difficulties may be of relatively minor concern.

Strict sterility must be the rule in treatment tanks because of the absence of those balancing factors which help to make the 'natural' system work. For this reason, uneaten food and waste products should be siphoned out once a day at least, to avoid additional bacterial infections. Despite this need for sterility, we have not as yet found any necessity for the use of ozonifiers, filters, etc.

We do not like to keep our stock solutions for too long, especially in the case of copper sulphate as it tends to go cloudy and we believe that the effectiveness may be reduced.

A period of recuperation and observation is normally necessary after the cure of the more serious diseases and convalescent fishes should be carefully protected from aggressors and from further infection. Nor should they be left to contend for food against stronger, healthier companions. A fish which has been injured by bullying must not be put back into the same tank as its tormentor.

So far as invertebrates are concerned, their main enemies are predators, although we presume that they have their own peculiar diseases and parasites. Possibly they may also play host to parasites which at a later stage of existence can afflict the fishes (as is the case with some freshwater snails in Europe and with the Chinese liver fluke).

We have no evidence, however, that this is the case. So far as our experience goes, invertebrates do not need preventive treatment against fish ailments. Nor do they appear to act as carriers of any of the more common fish diseases beyond the fourteen-day period (if at all).

Even in the case of serious tank infections such as *Oodinium,* they will not require treatment. In such a case, all the fishes should be removed to a treatment tank and in the absence of fish hosts the parasites will die out during the quarantine period of fourteen days. Meanwhile, no fishes should be put into the infected tank and, if fresh seawater is readily available, a water change will naturally give the cured fishes the best possible chance of full recovery.

An isolated outbreak of fungus in a newly purchased fish does not warrant a water change. However, if there should be any further out-breaks, a partial change should be carried out.

Diseases such as tail and fin rot often stem from fighting caused by overcrowding, incompatibility of certain fishes, too few refuges or inadequate escape routes. Never put a cured fish back into the tank until you feel certain that you have traced and removed the cause of its sickness.

Common diseases

Fishes are prey to a surprising number of diseases and disorders, but in our tanks we have only experienced *Oodinium,* tail and fin rot, wasting disease and physical injuries and even of these we have had relatively few cases. This is probably because most of our fishes are caught with hand nets and brought straight from the sea into 'natural' system tanks. Furthermore, we do not have the complications caused by cold and draughts. Most of the sickness which we have witnessed has taken place in our quarantine tanks and we very strongly recommend the use of such tanks as these will reduce the chance of attacks in established tanks to a minimum.

Many aquarists in Europe or America will be more knowledgeable about fish diseases than we are, but we hope that our experience and comments with regard to *Oodinium* may prove useful, as we feel that 90 per cent of marine fish fatalities stem from this infection.

Information on marine fish diseases is very scanty, although those of freshwater fishes and some marine diseases are extensively covered in a book by C. van Duijn Jnr, *Diseases of Fishes,* the first edition of which was written in 1956. (A second extended edition appeared in 1967.) It is interesting to note that in 1956 he was already recommending methylene blue as an effective cure for *Oodinium.* Much of the information in this chapter, where our own experience is lacking, is drawn from the second edition of Van Duijn's book.

Gill diseases

Most of the nitrogenous wastes from the life processes of fishes are discharged through the gills rather than through the urinary tract. This is particularly so in the case of marine fishes due to osmotic pressures. Gills, therefore, are vital to the disposal of toxic wastes in addition to their more generally-known function of extracting oxygen from the water. Damage to the gills of marine fishes is even more harmful than similar damage to their freshwater counterparts.

59

Although it is likely that marine fishes are just as subject to gill flukes, parasitic copepods, gill worms, etc., as freshwater fishes, these are of relatively little importance compared to *Oodinium*.

Oodinium. This disease is generally known as *Oodinium* or coral fish disease. It is caused by a protozoan parasite *Oodinium ocellatum* belonging to the dinoflagellates. It was discovered in 1934 by E. M. Brown and later it was demonstrated to be identical with the organism described as *Branchiophilus maris* found by Schäperclaus in 1935.

The parasite encysts and reproduces rapidly. In the sea the disease may be of little concern to a fish, as the offspring will be discharged into the water over a wide area and the chance of reinfection is slight. In a tank, however, there is no escape from exceptionally heavy reinfection, which the fish is in no way conditioned to withstand. In the sea, *Oodinium* is probably of no more serious consequence to a fish than a common cold is to a human – within the confines of a tank it could be likened to pneumonia or worse.

Remedial action must be taken immediately the first symptoms are noted and *all* fishes within the tank concerned must be treated as infected, even those showing no signs of infection. The main attack of the parasite is against the gills and will only spread to the rest of the body when the gills are heavily infected. The fish will give first warning of the attack by gasping and rising to the surface and displaying signs of weakness and apathy. Urgent treatment is necessary as once serious damage is done to the gills recovery is unlikely. Heavy infection on the body may be a sign that the disease is too far advanced for cure. Obviously one should not abandon remedial measures in such cases and a remedy which fails to produce a cure should not be condemned as ineffective because treatment was undertaken too late.

Oodinium ocellatum is very similar in appearance and behaviour to its freshwater counterparts *Oodinium limneticum,* the cause of velvet disease in freshwater fishes and *Oodinium pillularis,* causing the related but more serious pillularis disease. These parasites have a free-swimming stage, using a long whiplike tail as a means of propulsion. They settle on the skin or gills of a fish producing outgrowths which penetrate the epithelium. These parasites are in the twilight dividing zone between plant and animal. They obtain most of their food from the epidermal cells of the host, but also receive a certain amount of nourishment by photosynthesis employing the chlorophyll within their own body. The chlorophyll gives a yellow or brown tinge to the parasite and the infected fish therefore appears to be covered with a dust similar to the palish yellow dust of velvet disease or the greyish dust of pillularis disease. When mature the parasite encysts *on* the skin of the fish and a series of equal divisions takes place within the cyst until several hundred new free-swimming parasites are discharged within a few days.

We are coming to the conclusion that some of the cysts may lie dormant for very long periods and only emerge under suitable conditions – such as shock, chemical changes in the water or the fish, or a sudden drop of temperature. Two very different cases lead us to this view.

Mr Lee Chin Eng mentioned that, collecting on a hot day, he had a good catch of fishes in his container floating on the surface of the sea when a sudden heavy thunderstorm took place, with a consequent drop in temperature. Just after this, he noticed that most of the fishes were covered with *Oodinium*.

The second case concerned a consignment of fishes which we sent to the U.K. from Singapore. These included a magnificent pair of cardinal clowns which had bred on two occasions. These were isolated in one bag and to avoid any risk we used water from their own tank in which they had lived for five to six months. From another tank we sent some blue demoiselles and some dascyllus which we believed to be breeding and several gobies which we knew to have spawned recently. These were also packed apart from other fishes and similar precautions were observed with the water. All the fishes had been in our possession for at least five to six months and we had taken extreme care to protect them from infection as we wished to determine whether the spawning urge would survive transportation. Upon arrival, all were suffering from *Oodinium* and the copper sulphate cure (in which, at that time, both we and the recipient of the fishes had much faith) failed to work. There seemed to be no reason why such specimens, dispatched in excellent health under textbook conditions, should arrive heavily infected. Unless, that is, they already contained the means of infection on their bodies, waiting to attack them as soon as the temperature changed or, perhaps, when their bodies suffered some chemical change induced by shock. At temperatures below 10 degrees Centigrade (50 degrees Fahrenheit) no reproduction of the parasites takes place, whereas between 10 degrees Centigrade and 20 degrees Centigrade (68 degrees Fahrenheit) the process is very slow. Optimal conditions for the development of the dinospores exist at *pH* 8·0, a density of the seawater of 1·012–1·021 and the presence of a relatively large amount of dissolved nitrates (final breakdown products of proteins), as mentioned by Van Duijn.

More recently, a major importer in England stated that in his opinion fishes received from overseas were invariably infected. He now starts remedial action immediately upon receipt, irrespective of appearances. This expert also stated that even a move of several hundred feet could initiate the disease. His advice to his own customers was to treat all newly purchased fishes for *Oodinium* before placing them in the ultimate community tank. From our own experience, there is a great deal of evidence to support this recommendation.

We have found no proof of the assertion that anemones assist in reducing the incidence of *Oodinium* in clowns. These fishes appear to be particularly susceptible to the disease whilst, as a general rule, brackish water fishes such as Malayan angels and scats, when kept in saltwater, seem to be among the most resistant.

Treatment with Methylene Blue: This remedy is not infallible, but if used in time will cure most cases. The product should be pure methylene blue of medical quality. The stock solution comprises 1 gram to 100 cubic centimetres of water. Add 4 cubic centimetres of stock solution per imperial gallon of water. This addition should be made in two doses of 2 cubic centimetres per imperial gallon, the second being added twenty-four hours after the first. The colour of the water after the second dose has been added should be very dark, so that the fishes are barely visible when more than six inches away from the front of the glass. The treatment tank should be completely clean and free from all organic matter or dirt. Any coal filter must be put out of operation since it would remove the dye rapidly from the water. Ordinary aeration is advised in cases of *Oodinium* infections, contrary to the policy advocated against saltwater ich. If the fishes appear to be short of oxygen, increase the aeration sufficiently to make them comfortable. The temperature of the water should be kept as *low* as the fishes will stand. The tank should be kept in darkness. Feeding should be limited to food which is immediately accepted by the fishes. Fish wastes and any uneaten food should be siphoned out once a day. The fishes must be kept in the solution for at least ten days after the second dose has been added. If they are then clear of the disease, they can be removed to untreated water and kept under observation for a further four to five days before returning to the community tank. The fishes should be kept under close observation during treatment and aeration increased if any signs of undue distress appear.

The Action of Methylene Blue: The methylene blue acts on the

Oodinium ocellatum parasite in two ways. The heavy blue colour cuts out red light rays – this will reduce photosynthesis to negligible proportions and thus prevent development of the motile (palmella) stage. Methylene blue will also directly attack the parasite whilst it is free swimming and whilst it is on the fish. Unlike the *Ichthyopthirius* parasite, *O. ocellatum* is not covered completely by the epidermis of its host making it susceptible to immediate effects of chemicals. When attacked by methylene blue, the parasite will not mature and encyst normally, but will gradually be killed.

Treatment with Copper Sulphate: When using copper sulphate we find that the best prescription is one recommended by Mr Lee Chin Eng, as this gives us positive control of the final dose, whereas liquid solutions purchased already made up in the minute concentrations required may be subject to error.

Stock solution: 1 gram of copper sulphate to 1 litre of water. (Get your chemist to measure out a few 1-gram packets, making sure *that each one gram is weighed out separately,* instead of weighing the bulk mass and dividing it over the packets 'on sight' as is sometimes done when preparing powders.) Add 1 cubic centimetre of stock solution for every litre of water, but administer this in three equal doses over twenty-four hours. For example, a 60-litre tank would require the first dose (20 cubic centimetres) of stock mixture at say 9 a.m., the second at 9 p.m. and the third at 8.30 a.m. the next morning.

When using copper sulphate watch for signs of shock in the fishes and if distress appears slow down the rate of application. *Chelmon rostratus* are particularly sensitive in this respect. Treatment will, of course, be carried out in a separate clean tank and it is particularly important that not the slightest trace of copper sulphate comes into contact with the community tank, as it is deadly to most invertebrates – particularly corals and anemones. Full normal aeration must be given and the fishes should not be fed during treatment. They should be kept in the solution for a period of four days by which time the disease should have disappeared. During this time any fish wastes must be siphoned off. If the fishes appear clear by the end of the fourth day, remove them from the treatment tank and keep them under observation in quarantine for a further ten days, using new untreated seawater and resume feeding. Do not return to the main tank until that tank has had the full resting period of fourteen days for any parasites to die out.

The Action of Copper Sulphate: The action of copper sulphate is to increase the formation of mucus on the body of the fish. Surplus mucus is sloughed off including, presumably, the semi-embedded parasites. The parasites rapidly die when free swimming or when removed from the host and exposed to the full action of the chemical. Copper is fatal to most forms of animal life, including fishes, if the concentration is too strong.

Copper sulphate unfortunately does produce varying results: in some cases complete and swift recovery, in others complete failure. We suspect that this variation in results – even when it is used under apparently identical conditions – is due to there being different forms of the parasite. Since we are not in a position to determine which form of parasite is concerned, we prefer the slower but more generally reliable methylene blue treatment.

Other treatments for Oodinium: Other treatments available include acriflavine, quinine salts and some antibiotics. We do not feel, however, that any of these are superior to the cures recommended earlier, and some have the disadvantage that they may induce sterility or other harmful side-effects such as vitamin deficiency. We have recently heard about some promising new proprietary cures but have not yet had an opportunity of trying these. The important point with any such medicine is, of course, to observe most strictly the manufacturer's instructions as shown on the label and not to allow the product to come into contact with any invertebrates, whether or not there is a printed warning to this effect.

Heat treatment: An even simpler cure was reported to us during a recent visit to East Africa. An aquarist who exports marine fishes from the Mombasa area stated that she frequently encountered *Oodinium* but had found a heat treatment which was effective. The procedure is simple. The tank should be darkened and the temperature raised slowly to 90 degrees Fahrenheit. After a short time at this temperature, the water should be allowed to drop to normal temperature. Aeration should naturally be very strong to compensate for the drop in oxygen tension. This treatment has to be carried out on two successive days, after which the fishes are said to be clear of infection.

If the method is as effective in areas other than East Africa, it will certainly be a great boon to all aquarists. Indeed, it might be possible to carry out the treatment in the community tanks, provided that the resi-

12. *Coris gaimard.* The beautiful humped coral has corallites similar to those of *Polyphyllia talpina* but the tentacles are more robust and are constantly extended. It is a most satisfactory coral – probably a species of *Polyphyllia*
   Photograph by the author

13. Golden wrasse swimming over a coral of the *Herpolitha* species – probably a distorted *H. limax*
   Photograph by the author

14. Harlequin fish *Lepidoplois mesothorax*. Note also fingers of pink sponge
    Photograph by the author

15. The dark fish is a Bird wrasse in typical bird-like posture
    Photograph by the author

dent invertebrates are capable of withstanding the abnormal temperatures involved.

Conclusion: It is clear that there is still a great deal to learn about the various forms of this disease. The speed with which a fatal attack can develop is frightening and we have reason to believe from personal experience that cysts may lie dormant for long periods and then be activated by shock or changes in temperature or body chemistry. The variation in the length of time for recovery, ranging from two days for the heat cure to ten days for methylene blue, is perplexing.

Chances of a cure are reasonable with known remedies provided that treatment is undertaken soon enough. On the basis that prevention is better than cure, however, there appears to be a very good case for applying prophylactic treatment upon receipt of newly purchased stock, particularly if this includes clowns. Fish which you are able to catch for yourself direct from the sea should not need such treatment.

Saltwater Ich (Ichthyopthirius). We cannot speak with first-hand knowledge of this disease as we have had no outbreaks in our own marine tanks. This is odd, as we have in the past had many outbreaks of the freshwater form amongst various species of *Rasbora* which we used to collect in Malaysia and Indonesia. Our information is of necessity drawn from reports by Van Duijn and other sources.

There are significant differences between this disease and *Oodinium*. The young free-swimming parasite becomes completely embedded within the skin of the fish by proliferation of the epithelium. The white spots visible are not the parasite, but additional epithelial cells formed by the fish to combat irritation caused by the parasite which feeds on the red blood corpuscles of the host. When mature, the parasite leaves the fish and sinks to the bottom forming a jellylike cyst – in this it again differs from *Oodinium* of which the cyst is formed on the skin of the fish. Reproduction within the cyst is approximately four to five times more prolific than that of the *Oodinium* parasite and up to 1,200 new individuals can develop from one adult.

For this disease the use of methylene blue is recommended in nearly the same way as for *Oodinium* and for the same period. However, in this case only coarse bubble aeration near the water surface is allowed, since the effect on ich partly depends on lowering of the oxygen content of the water, from which the fishes do not suffer because methylene blue adsorbed in their tissues acts as a substitute respiratory substance, acting

E

like haemoglobin. Further, the temperature should not be lower than 21 to 26 degrees Centigrade (70 to 80 degrees Fahrenheit) or as near to this as the fish will stand.

Quinine hydrochloride is stated to be a useful alternative cure in freshwater, but as this depends for its best effects on a *pH* of 6·5 and seawater is normally much more alkaline than freshwater, there are problems in reducing the *pH* and in its actual measurement. We feel, therefore, that it is better to rely upon methylene blue which is safer, more reliable and much simpler to use.

Tail and Fin Rot. We find this second in importance to *Oodinium* as a lethal disease.

The infection is of bacterial origin and usually attacks fins damaged by accidents, trapping or fighting. Our own cases have mostly occurred in fishes bought recently from the market. The action is very rapid and if the tail rots down to the caudal peduncle death is certain. Immediate treatment is necessary and the disease would seem to be infectious in some cases.

We would only try surgery as a very last resort as in most cases we have found treatment with iodine and antibiotics to be effective, provided that it is started soon enough. Our usual practice is to use a dilute solution of iodine followed by aureomycin.

Treatment with Iodine and Aureomycin: Touch the infected parts gently with a cotton-wool stick or a soft-haired brush dipped in a solution of 1:10 parts of commercial iodine solution (10 per cent in ethanol) to water, taking great care not to touch portions other than those infected: gills and eyes should never be touched with this solution. After treatment, allow the fish to recover for a time either in the water of its own tank or in another aerated container of seawater. After the shock of this treatment has diminished, place the fish in a clean tank with aureomycin.

We find that an effective solution of this drug is 250 milligrams per four imperial (five U.S.) gallons of seawater. The capsules usually supplied for medical purposes contain 250 milligrams. Mixing with seawater should naturally be carried out in a separate container before decanting the solution into the treatment tank.

Treatment should not be continued for more than three to four days and the bacteria should be completely destroyed well within that time. The fins should have started to grow. We recommend that the affected fish then be kept in a convalescent tank – possibly the treatment tank itself refilled with new seawater – until it has recovered sufficiently to look after itself.

If you wish initially to use a stronger solution than that recommended above, because of the severity of the damage, then the period of treatment should be reduced. You may increase the dosage by 50 per cent and decrease the period accordingly. Some experts recommend an even stronger mixture with no decrease in the period, but we consider this hazardous. Do not try a longer period with a weaker solution, because this may not kill all the bacteria and those which survive may create resistant strains; in addition there may be possible side-effects on the fish.

We sometimes receive relatively large unusual fishes which have been caught in the fishermen's traps. These are often extensively damaged and ragged from their efforts to escape. In such a case, we cut out the first part of the cure (iodine followed by a rest) and put them straight into aureomycin 50 per cent stronger than that recommended for normal use. In such a case, when not using iodine, we employ some of the aureomycin from the total dose and apply a strong mixture of this mixed with seawater to the affected parts (as with iodine, eyes and gills should not be touched). Application is made by means of a cotton-wool stick or a soft-haired brush. This strong solution applied directly to the fish will wash off into the water of the treatment tank and allowance should be made accordingly by reducing the dose put directly into the tank to take account of that already on the fish.

There is another antibiotic – achromycin – which we have also applied in the same way and with the same dosage and we also find this effective. All antibiotics, however, carry the risk of side-effects and in no circumstances should treatment last longer than the periods recommended. Some experts consider that fishes being so treated should receive supplementary vitamins with their food. Aureomycin is known to cause a deficiency in vitamins of the B-complex (especially B12), together with vitamins E and K.

Van Duijn generally recommends the use of chloromycetin instead of aureomycin for treatment of fish diseases, at a rate of 13 milligrams per litre (60 milligrams per imperial gallon). In cases of tail and fin rot he recommends that the treatment be combined with feeding the fish with a suitable food to which 1 milligram per gram of food has been added. For fishes of at least 10 grams of weight the dosage may be increased to 50 milligrams per litre for up to 24 hours only. However, this applies to experiments with freshwater fishes and has still to be corroborated for marines.

Wasting Disease. This is an infection that from our experience appears to be confined to the clowns – particularly *Amphiprion percula*. To date we have found no effective remedy. A photograph of an infected fish appears facing page 16.

In the early stages of this disease, the fish behaves normally – both those in the photograph are performing in characteristic manner. A little later, however, a sick fish will forsake its anemone and shimmy miserably, often in a corner of the tank and it will appear to lose interest in food.

After this death comes relatively suddenly: to date we have had no recoveries. There are no obvious signs of wastage or internal parasites. None of the usual cures such as methylene blue, copper sulphate, or antibiotics will have any effect upon it. We are still looking for other remedies.

This disease appears to be either infectious or contagious amongst all clown fishes, but strangely enough it does not seem to affect other genera. There were many fishes other than *Amphiprion* in the tank in which the photograph was taken and these were in no way affected.

The only advice which we can offer at this stage is to remove any fish so affected as quickly as possible to a separate tank in the hope that this will prevent infection of the remaining *Amphiprion*.

The infection is fortunately not common. We have as yet been unable to find any record of this disease elsewhere. One major distributor of marine fishes in the U.K. confirmed having had fishes with such an infection and similar lack of success in finding a cure.

Wounds or Injuries. Minor wounds are better left alone, but the victim or its aggressor should be removed to another tank. We find that normally healthy fishes in a well-cared-for tank will heal on their own and we feel that the shock caused by chasing and capturing them may be more harmful than the minor injury to be treated. Major injuries, especially those in newly acquired specimens, are a different matter as they may also be incubating tail and fin rot. Such fishes should receive the iodine and/or aureomycin treatment as recommended earlier.

Fungus Infections – Family Saprolegniaceæ. There are a great many members of this plant family. Although different forms of the infection can develop, the overall treatment is the same. Fungus growing in the tank will not necessarily attack fishes but may live on organic matter alone. If it does attack a weakened fish, the results may be fatal.

The fungus consists of two parts – the external threads called hyphae and their lower thinner parts which grow into the substratum (e.g. the skin of a fish) – the mycelium. Killing the former is easy, but the latter is more difficult to destroy, as it is protected by the skin of the fish. The main action of the fungus is to cause degeneration of the skin cells and muscles, but it can also penetrate to the skeleton if neglected.

This infection is unlikely to attack healthy fishes and is usually found in those which have been weakened by injuries from fighting, by other diseases or by being kept in badly maintained tanks. As it produces freely motile spores, it is possible that it can be transmitted from other tanks. We have not yet had an active case in our marine tanks.

Treatment for Fungus. Prevention is the best policy. Fishes with injuries from fighting or those which are suffering from the after-effects of a serious infection such as *Oodinium* should not be returned to the main tanks until fully recovered and feeding normally.

From Van Duijn's recommendations for treatment of infections involving small areas in freshwater fishes, *but not for preparing treatment baths*, we have derived the following adaptations for sea fishes:

(a) Iodine: 1 part of commercial iodine solution (10 per cent in ethanol) with 9 parts of seawater.
(b) Mercurochrome 1 part of 2 per cent solution of mercurochrome mixed with 9 parts of seawater.
(c) Merthiolate 1 part of merthiolate mixed with 999 parts of seawater.
(d) Dichromate of Potash (Potassium dichromate) 1 per cent solution. This solution is the weakest of the four but most suitable for very small or delicate fishes.

Whichever remedy is preferred, it is recommended that the head and gills of the fish be kept under water and the infected place touched with a brush or cotton-wool swab dipped into it. Ensure that healthy places are untouched. After this, the fish should be put into a sterile tank with potassium dichromate to a strength of between 1:20,000 or 1:25,000, i.e. 1 gram to 5 or 6 imperial gallons. Treatment should continue for seven to ten days or until recovery, whichever is the earlier; longer treatment can have injurious effects. The water must be well aerated, and it is advisable to raise the temperature several degrees. After treatment, the water must be changed completely.

Warning: No references are available as to the effect of this treatment on seawater animals and plants in general! Treatment should therefore be confined to heavily infected fishes only. It should not be carried out in a main tank, as is allowed in freshwater aquaria.

Shock and Poisoning. Marine specimens come straight from the wild, whereas a large proportion of freshwater aquarium fishes are bred in captivity. Marines consequently have much the greater problem of adjustment to tank conditions, particularly as most of them will only have been out of the sea for a few weeks by the time that they reach their final home. Such thoughtless actions as the sudden switching on of tank lights in a dark room, rapping on the glass and unnecessary handling can be terrifying to a half-wild fish. We have known at least one *Chelmon rostratus* to die from shock or fright – these particular fish are especially nervous.

Provide plenty of hiding-places, caves and crannies where initially nervous fishes can hide and feel secure. If you are compelled to empty your tanks – do not chase the fishes all around the corals. Quietly remove the largest pieces and uncover the hiding-places, then take out such fishes as can readily be caught, and continue the process progressively before really commencing to stir up the tank. Remember that a sick or injured fish is liable to be particularly susceptible to shock.

Poisoning is due to defective tank conditions or to tanks of unsuitable material or design and has been covered elsewhere. Fishes which are suffering from general tank poisoning should be given as ideal conditions as possible in which to recuperate and care should be taken not to expose them to further infections (nor to aggressors) whilst in their weakened condition.

Eye ailments. We have only slight experience with troubles of this nature and all these have been fairly minor.

There are occasions when one eye swells and becomes uncomfortably large. Very often this is due to too bright lighting and can be cured by moving the fish to a darker tank or providing more shade. Much the same type of trouble can be caused by the eye being knocked against coral, but such injuries are usually self-curing.

If spots or an almost fungus like growth start to appear in the eye, we find that the aureomycin treatment recommended for tail and fin rot is often effective. Aureomycin (and also chloromycetin) can be applied directly to the eye, just as is done in human eye infections but we just let

70

the fish swim about in the treatment tank containing the prescribed dose.

Conclusion

Provided that due care is exercised on receipt of the fishes, that they are properly quarantined and cared for, outbreaks of disease should be comparatively rare.

There are many other diseases not discussed in this chapter, but we believe that we have covered those most likely to concern the average aquarist.

6. Collecting

We will not describe in detail the methods of collecting all the various marine creatures. Such information could only be of interest to relatively few of our readers, i.e. those who have access to suitable reefs as well as the time and patience to spend in collecting and quarantining their own specimens. For the sake of these few we are including the following brief notes.

But first of all we would make two pleas: Do not take from the reef more specimens than you can accommodate and keep healthy in a community tank.

When you turn over a piece of rock or coral please remember to replace it exactly in its original position, and the same way up. If you forget to do this all the smaller creatures which can only live beneath the shelter of the rock will die.

The question of tank preparation is dealt with in our chapter on Tank Arrangement which also gives more detailed suggestions as to suitable contents. The safest possible tank for a beginner to start with would be one devoted mainly to anemones and clowns. For a 36 × 15 × 18-inches tank we would suggest, in addition to a liberal supply of coral rock and a layer of sand, two 6 to 8-inch anemones and two pairs of clowns. A small amount of live coral would be safe, say four or five pieces, none above 4 inches in size. One or two sand corals such as *Fungia* could be added but these should be smaller. A few tube worms, small cowries, shrimps and sea squirts would help to make the tank attractive and the cowries and shrimps would make good scavengers. So also would a few brittle stars, but these should not be too large. There is no need to collect worms as these will certainly be present in the rock. Do not include crabs as these would be liable to damage the corals and tube worms. Molluscs and sponges should be avoided until you have more experience. Do not use anemones unless you are including clowns and do not have clowns without anemones.

Be very firm with yourself at first: coral taken straight from the wild is unpredictable and you should not experiment with any but the safest of the 'safe' corals listed in this book. Avoid any with sponge or other life growing upon it. Prod gently into any crevices to determine whether they are filled with sponge and tap the coral lightly. If it sounds hollow you may find that the cavity is filled with sponge. Hump-shaped corals such as some species of *Goniopora* and *Favia* are particularly suspect in this respect. You should also sniff the coral to detect the presence of rotting matter. But remember that this will not tell you whether it contains living sponge liable to die off when it gets into your tank. *Then* it will start to smell.

Do not pile corals one upon the other in the collecting buckets nor let them touch each other with their nematocysts. Similarly, they must be kept out of reach of the tentacles of *Cerianthus* and anemones. Never keep any of your specimens out of water and do not leave them unshaded in the sunlight for any length of time. If it is not possible to keep coral rock completely covered, protect the unsubmerged part with seaweed and make sure that the seaweed is kept damp. Change the water frequently whilst on the reef and for the last time immediately prior to the journey home, but NOT at the quayside unless the inshore water is absolutely clear of contamination.

Fish should not be put into the same collecting bucket as any large or particularly sharp pieces of coral which are liable to fall about and damage them, but they need some coral in their buckets to keep them from panicking.

It is possible to limit your collecting to the invertebrates and to buy fishes from dealers or local fishermen. The problem with such fishes is that they are liable to be diseased due to overcrowding in the fish bins, or to damage incurred in traps. We do not like using trapped fish, but prefer those which have been caught with a hand-net. Most of the fishermen use traps but it is sometimes possible to persuade them to lift their traps shortly after they have been put down and in this way to avoid most of the damage which comes from too long imprisonment and the fish fighting each other in their attempts to get free. Another method is to persuade some of the local boys to dive down amongst the anemones and bring you up a pair of clowns.

Anemones must not be pulled off the rocks as this damages the pedal disc. Once it is torn the creature has to be returned to the water where it may recover – the chances of it surviving in a tank in a damaged condition are slight. In the case of anemone *Radianthus,* a sand anemone, this is best collected whilst still attached to the small rock to which it is holding beneath the sand. Rock anemones usually exert too tight a hold to dislodge immediately. If the rock is not too large they should be lifted whilst still on their rock and suspended head downwards over a bucket of seawater. In ten minutes or so the anemone will start to show gaps between the pedal disc and the rock and a fingernail can then gently be inserted which may make it possible to prise away the anemone. Do not choose the largest anemones: these creatures are greedy for aeration and an expanded diameter of 6 to 8 inches is big enough for a start.

If collecting tube worms, be very careful not to damage the tube. Should this become torn, put the creature back amongst the rocks where it may recover or grow a new tube. The type with soft parchment-like tubes may be removed from their rock by gently peeling the sheath away from the rock. They will re-establish themselves on another piece of your choice provided that it has suitable crevices. Do not attempt to collect those with large calcareous tubes.

When collecting sand and coral rock it is important to preserve the myriad living creatures contained within by keeping both rock and sand damp until you can get them home and into aerated water. They should preferably be kept under water in the collecting buckets, but size and weight may prevent this. Covering them with damp seaweed will help.

Another point with regard to sand is that it is best taken from a sand-bar washed by fast-running tides. Such sand will comprise a high proportion of pounded down shells and being relatively coarse will be of a suitable quality. Finer sand is undesirable, nor should it ever be sifted. We only take the top $\frac{1}{4}$ to $\frac{1}{2}$ an inch of surface sand, scraping it up carefully with our hands, as soon as possible after the sandbar starts to show with the falling tide.

Seawater is best collected some distance from shore, particularly if the coast is muddy. Even with muddy water the sediment will settle out after standing, however, and the water itself is likely to be rich in plankton. Water contaminated by industrial effluents, sewage, oil or freshwater (as in the case of estuaries) should be avoided. Use plastic bags or rigid plastic containers for collecting it because any form of rust or metal corrosion is a potential hazard.

To avoid the risk of introducing parasites harmful to the fishes it may be desirable that seawater should be quarantined before use. If you have the storage facilities to keep it for ten to fourteen days before putting it into your fish tanks you will reduce the risk of infection from this source. (We have not been able to assess the extent of this risk, but our limited experience suggests that it may not be very great.) *Oodinium* parasites, for example, will die out within this period if they have no host fishes to infect. If there are no fishes in the tank and you do not propose to add any within the next fourteen days, there is no point in quarantining the water.

There are two methods of treating water in quarantine. One is to keep the water in the original container for the period, in which event all the life in the water will have died and it will be virtually sterile. The other, which we prefer, is to preserve at least some of the plankton content by putting the water into an empty tank and keeping it aerated. If space is short there is no reason why it should not be put into the same tank as new corals, invertebrates and plants also undergoing quarantine. The only drawback to this arrangement is that if any of the other creatures die they may contaminate the water.

Setting up a tank with creatures taken straight from the reef is far more difficult than merely maintaining one which has been bought from an expert and therefore, we hope, properly planned, quarantined and acclimatized. But it is much more satisfying.

Equipment

The equipment required for collecting is basically simple, comprising:

(a) 'Snorkel' mask. The type usually recommended as being the safest is that with separate eye-piece and mouth-tube. This is most unlikely to let you down and is said to be easy to use after a little practice. Some authorities consider that it is the only safe type, especially for children, who may panic if a valve jams. We do not like breathing through our mouths and use an Italian mask with one built-in tube and a valve.

SCUBA equipment is not strictly necessary as you do not need to dive more than 15 to 20 feet at the most. A neoprene tunic of the type worn by SCUBA divers is, however, ideal if you intend to spend long periods in the water. Not only does it give protection against the cold but also reduces the risk of stings.

(b) Footwear. Never go on to the reef, or even the reef flats, without adequate footwear. Apart from the more obvious hazards such as stonefish, sea urchins and similar creatures, the reef is very sharp to bare feet. Flippers are admirable for fast swimming but are extremely clumsy on the jagged edge of the reef and it is impossible to walk on the coral in them. We use strong rubber-soled tennis shoes. They do not impede

swimming and give a reasonable degree of protection. It is unlikely that they would provide complete security if you were to step squarely upon a stonefish. They would, however, mitigate the degree of poisoning which is dependent on the depth of penetration and the amount of poison injected. For this reason the stouter the sole the better, provided that it does not unduly impair swimming ability.

(c) Nets. We usually carry two wire-handled bat-shaped nets. The net itself measures 10 inches across at the broadest part and is 12 inches long by about 20 inches deep. We like to have our nets made so that the fabric does not come to a point at the bottom – they are better with a basin-shaped bottom which makes it easier to extricate the fishes. The bat-shaped frame has a straight edge at the top, i.e. opposite the handle. This is an advantage because it can be placed flush with the ground when you want to shoo a fish into your other net and block off its way of escape; it is also easier for poking into the coral. For the netting itself we use a green garden screening material with a small mesh. Most of the nets sold in the local shops are unsuitable because the mesh is usually too large and the aluminium frame unable to withstand the effects of saltwater. If you buy your nets readymade and are at all uncertain about their ability to withstand the tearing effect of coral, it is best to take a needle and thread on every expedition. Nothing is more frustrating than having a good tide for fishing but unserviceable nets. If more than one person is fishing, a net of 8 to 10 feet in length with a depth of 6 feet or so is also useful. This should be weighted with a light chain along one lengthwise edge and should have small floats sewn on the parallel edge. (This will make a floating 'fence' 6 feet high.) It can be used in deeper water with a sandy bottom. The net is spread to make a horseshoe-shaped enclosure, and fast-moving fish such as cleaner wrasses can be herded into it after which the gap is closed and the fish caught by diving into the enclosed area with hand-nets.

(d) Knife. We find a stainless steel knife, which is made in Spain and is much used by skin-divers, to be very useful. This has a screwdriver tip and one edge is serrated. There is a garter-type holster by which it can be attached to the leg, but we find that it is easier to work with the holster slung from a waist belt.

(e) Containers. The containers used for the collection should be of plastic and it is best to have assorted shapes and sizes, the largest being

76

baby's bath size. These containers should be reserved for fish collecting and fish treatments and should never be allowed to come into contact with soap, detergents, insecticides, disinfectants or other chemicals, except perhaps for the occasional use of methylene blue or permanganate of potash. If they have previously been used for treating sick fishes they must be sterilized before use. For collecting water you need 5-gallon plastic jerricans which must never be used for any other purpose. Make sure that they are new and unused when you buy them.

Boating

If you are only going to collect a few specimens occasionally it will be cheaper for you to hire a boat and a man to handle it. Should you be thinking of buying a boat, however, the following points may be useful:

Twin engines are to be preferred. With two engines you do not have to change a sheer pin in deep water and a choppy sea, nor do you face the risk of being stranded for hours if one engine fails to start.

Ensure that your boat has sufficient room to house water containers and the specimens which you will be collecting without causing too much congestion and remember that you will need some protection from the sun both for yourself and your specimens.

The choice of a boat is very much a question of personal preference. Our own *Kingfisher* is a 20-foot half-cabin cruiser powered by twin 28-horsepower outboard motors, plank built and of robust construction. She has a canvas awning over the open section aft and this protects us and our collections from the very strong sunlight.

Personal safety

General seamanship is well covered in a number of books relating to power craft. A good look-out and forward thinking should enable you to avoid most hazards. Do not forget to carry a torch, toolkit, spare sheer pins (if used on your engine), reserve drinking water, matches, lifejackets for the children and first-aid kit.

Your doctor is the best person to consult as to the contents of the first-aid box, with special reference to the more vicious of the local bites and stings. He can also tell you which injuries are likely to need an anti-tetanus injection.

Obtain a tide table for your area. These useful publications show the times and heights of high and low water and may save you from being stranded by the occasional exceptionally low tides. They will also help you to plan your collecting trips for the best times of the day, i.e. around low water.

You should also get good charts and study them carefully. Areas with particularly dangerous currents are invariably marked and Admiralty charts usually specify the nature of the foreshore – whether it is sand, mud or coral. This can save a lot of time which might otherwise be wasted exploring a part of the coast where there is no coral.

Always note the direction of current and wind when approaching a reef. It will pay you to switch into neutral to observe the drift a few yards out before finally committing yourself to a landing. When you do go in, do not go too fast – there may be an unexpected coral head just below the waterline. We usually reverse to bring the boat to a standstill then, after going into neutral, very gently edge into forward gear on one engine. If the wind and tide are setting towards the reef, do not go in unless you are very sure that you can get off again, but try the other side of the reef.

When on the reef, watch the currents carefully. These can change in both direction and strength very rapidly. During the spring tides in particular, if the reefs are extensive, the tides can run between them very swiftly indeed, as a large volume of water pours through a relatively narrow channel. Exposure of some sections of a reef as the tide ebbs will suddenly cause the current to change direction and the same thing can happen when the tide floods in again. Drifts often run from shallow to deeper water and the current can sometimes be so strong that it is necessary to cling to the rocks to keep a footing, even in shallow water. On other days the same part of the reef may have perfectly calm water.

You need to know what to do in an emergency. If the strap of your snorkel breaks or loosens, or the valve jams under water – the easiest thing to do is to surface, tear off the mask, roll on to your back and either float or use an easy back stroke until you reach shallow water.

No one should swim or dive unattended and ideally no one should walk on the reef alone for fear that sudden disabling injuries may lead to drowning. The risk of such injury comes not only from dangerous animals but also from breaking coral which may trap a foot or an ankle.

Dangerous Creatures

There are some dangerous animals in all tropical waters, but a little foreknowledge will enable you to avoid most of these risks. You should learn to recognize the harmful animals in your own collecting area, how to avoid them, and the recommended first-aid measures.

Information on these matters is usually easy to obtain from the local people and there is also a very useful book on the subject, *Dangerous Marine Animals,* by Bruce W. Halstead. We list below some of the more common hazards.

Sharks and Barracuda. Avoid swimming in waters which these creatures are known to frequent and keep away from shipping lanes and harbours (to which they are attracted by ships' garbage). Do not swim in deep cloudy water or in half light such as that at dawn and dusk. If you observe these precautions you may very well never see a shark or barracuda.

Sea snakes. These are gentle creatures and not aggressive, but dangerous if stepped upon. Do not wade through half-submerged weed beds. There should be no danger when swimming in deep water. If you should be bitten seek expert medical attention immediately – the effects of sea snake bite are not always immediately apparent, but the poison is extremely dangerous.

Stonefish. Found on reefs and even on sandbars, often in very shallow water – especially in wind-ruffled water, they look like algae-covered stones. Strong protective footwear and care when walking is the best safeguard. If you are injured, the pain will be sudden and intense. Fresh urine (as for a lion-fish sting) once cured a slight but painful injury caused to the author when he brushed a small stonefish with his hand. Do not rely on this method, however, other than as a palliative. The cure might not have worked had the creature been larger and trodden upon so that the spines had penetrated deeply.

Lion fishes. These are mainly found in deeper water or lurking under rocks or in caves on the deep-water edge of the reef. Never explore such crannies with bare hands – if you must investigate them use a long stick or the handle of your net. The injury causes sudden shooting pain. Fresh urine applied to the wound is reported to be used frequently in the Macassar area of Indonesia where these fish are common. Nothing is lost by adopting this treatment as a palliative measure whilst still seeking expert assistance as quickly as possible.

Moray eels. Found in crevices just below the level of the lowest tides or under rocks, they are not normally aggressive; if you avoid poking around crevices with bare hands and are careful where you put your feet you are unlikely to get bitten. We have had only one attack in five years and the creature was provoked in that instance.

Large Medusae. As these creatures are tide-borne there is little advice we can offer about avoiding them. If you see one you should keep well clear of it and make sure that you are in a position where the current cannot bring it towards you. Never touch any jellyfish – not even an apparently dead one washed up on the sand. *Physalia,* the Portugese man-of-war is widely distributed but the incidence of reported attacks in our area is small. We have no experience of the very lethal Australian sea wasp.

Venomous gastropods. Some members of the cone family (Conidae) are particularly lethal. Their shells are prized by collectors for the striking colours and patterns, but the predatory habits of these creatures, particularly at night, make them unsuitable for tank use. The poison is injected by the radula. Fortunately, in the daytime at least, these creatures are relatively sluggish. Do not pick them up by hand: if you wish to examine them you should use a collecting net.

Medical assistance required. The dangerous creatures listed in the foregoing paragraphs all inflict potentially lethal injuries and these call for the most urgent medical assistance. Never delay in getting this.

Sea urchins. Some are venomous, either because of venom contained in their spines or because they have the ability to inject poison by means of the pedicellariae, which are really small snapping pincers. The venomous ones can cause dangerous injuries and need immediate medical attention. Avoid all contact with sea urchins unless you are able to distinguish between the venomous and the harmless. Even the 'harmless' ones can cause a very great deal of pain if you fall into a bed of them, or if you tread upon one accidentally and because of the depth to which they can penetrate there is always the risk of infection.

Minor scourges

We only mention these because the literature about them is sparse. Anti-histamine cream, if applied immediately on a dry skin, is a very effective remedy for any minor pain or irritation.

80

Stinging corals. Millepora is the only type of coral found in our area which we know to have a sting which can be felt by human beings. No coral, coral rock, or seaweed should ever, however, be clasped to the body. It is not a question of the nematocysts of the coral, but rather of the minute stinging life living within or upon it. Wearing a shirt over your trunks or swimsuit is a useful protection, if you find that this does not hamper movement too much. A neoprene tunic is better. Gardening gloves with long gauntlets are useful to keep in the boat for the loading operation, because it is very difficult to lift a heavy piece of coral over the side of the boat without getting badly scratched.

Coral dust in the eye and coral cuts should never be neglected. Coral wounds are notoriously difficult to heal and will turn septic if not thoroughly cleansed immediately they happen.

Bristle worms. If you pick up enough pieces of coral you are bound to encounter traces of bristle worms, even if you do not see them. They are active segmented worms which live within or upon coral and coral rock. Fragile, glass-like bristles protrude from either side of these creatures, which look rather like flattened versions of the 'furry caterpillar'. The bristles can be readily discharged into anything which may touch them, particularly the fingers. They cause minor irritation, sometimes followed by a rash which is very persistent. It is almost impossible to brush off or pick out the bristles, but if the hands are immediately immersed in sea-water and vigorously rubbed together with a 'washing' movement the bristles will drop out. Keep the hands under water whilst 'washing' them. We do not say avoid collecting bristle worms: they are excellent tank scavengers and attractive-looking creatures.

Anemones. Few of the more common anemones will cause any noticeable stings to the hands, although some of the larger ones can inflict a mild sting, especially if allowed to brush against the back of the hand or any of the more sensitive parts of the body. An exception is *Stoichactis* which has short stubby tentacles. In these the nematocysts are potent. The tentacles feel sticky and readily detach themselves on to your person or on to the collecting net. The detached tentacles retain their stinging power for a long time. Do not, therefore, allow any left on the collecting net to touch the body, lest quite painful weals be formed.

Hydroids. The hydroids with which we are most familiar grow in col-onies in a graceful basket-like or fern-leaf form. Their colour is usually fawn or pale lilac. They can cause a painful rash, rather like nettle rash.

Planktonic animals. There are a number of minute planktonic animals, mostly of the medusa type, which can inflict a mild sting. These are mainly seasonal and much more common during the monsoon period when the water is cloudy.

7. Fishes

Fishes belong to the phylum Chordata and the class Pisces. Most of those suitable for an aquarium are found in the sub-class Actinopterygii or bony fishes. Fishes such as sharks and rays which have soft cartilaginous skeletons but no bones belong to the sub-class Euselachii.

All the fishes which we describe in these pages come from the Indo-Pacific.

Fascinating and healthy tanks can be achieved using only invertebrates and algae, but a tank without fishes is like a garden without birds; nor can it be considered truly 'natural'. Apart from this, waste products from the fishes help to breed useful bacteria to feed the lower forms of life.

We have concentrated upon those which are suitable for a domestic fish tank and have omitted any such as *Balistoides conspicillum* which, though handsome, are of little interest to a private collector because they need a very large aquarium. Others may be attractive in their juvenile form but lose their bright colours later. Gropers and snappers start life demurely as attractive small specimens but may finish by becoming rapacious monsters. We have not included such problem fishes in our list.

The family Pomacentridae contains a number of beautiful and adaptable fishes which will readily accept tank life: clown fishes, dascyllus and demoiselles. There are also lovely members of the Pomacanthidae and Chaetodontidae families, though some of the latter will eat coral. Wrasses (Labridae) tend to grow rather large but there are some excellent small ones and even the larger types are very well behaved and do not bully other fishes. These four families are the most important source of good tank fishes, but we have listed some from other families which are also satisfactory.

In order to add interest to a tank and as a contrast to the more glamorous specimens, it is useful to include a few 'personality fish'. One of our favourites was a grotesquely ugly little bottom-dweller whom we nicknamed 'Grandma Giles' because she looked so like the cartoon character. Another amusing fish is *Plectorhinchus chaetodonoides*. This has a bizarre arrangement of large spots and blotches in dark brown and white and moves with a distinctive wiggling motion of the whole body. It is never still, but continually exploring the rockwork. Even though it grows to a large size *P. chaetodonoides* remains extremely good tempered and does not harm other occupants of the tank.

When selecting fishes one must consider their eating habits and also their compatibility with each other and with other creatures. It is useless to attempt to keep *Trachyphyllia* or *Pocillopora* corals in the same tank as most Chaetodontidae. On the other hand, you could have *Turbinaria* or *Goniopora* in the same tank with these fishes and there would be no problem. Soft corals and small anemones will rapidly vanish if placed in the company of the larger batfishes (Platacidae) which also love to eat hydroids and similar animals. Parrot fishes (Scaridae) would welcome your choicer algae as a change of food and *Chelmon rostratus,* the butterfly fish, might amuse itself by pecking at the heads of tube worms and killing clams such as *Tridacna* which have wide open gapes. (This is a pity because alone of its family it will not damage coral and apart from this failing is well behaved.) Balistidae, the file or trigger fishes will also peck at tube worms.

The most thoroughly satisfactory all-round fishes are the clown fishes and the wrasses. Give clowns anemones to play in and wrasses sand under which to sleep at night, and they will cause no trouble except possibly to start an occasional fight over beats and territories with one of their own kind.

As in the case of freshwater fishes, there are some which will not survive in company with more vigorous companions. Razor fishes, pipe fishes and sea horses can only eat slow-moving live food and will starve if they have to compete for their meals with more active inhabitants. They are ideal for decorating tanks of the more delicate corals and tube worms which they cannot harm, as might more vigorous fishes.

We do not recommend keeping the following in a community tank: *Lagocephalidae* and *Tetraodontidae:* blowfishes and puffer fishes have sharp teeth and are fin nippers.
Antennariidae: frog fishes and sargassum fishes have large mouths and their camouflage makes it too easy for them to lie in wait for prey. We have known one to swallow a clown fish.
Synanceidae: stonefishes are dreaded even by the local fishermen. They make tank maintenance hazardous and can easily jump out if provoked.

Moreover they can live for some hours out of water and 'walk about' on the floor.

Scorpaenidae: We love these scorpion or lion fishes and the small ones are delicate and fascinating. However, the same objections apply to them as to the stonefishes and they are best kept in a separate tank.

Family Pomacentridae

The members of this family include: *Amphiprion* (clown fishes), *Dascyllus, Abudefduf* (demoiselles), *Chromis, Daya, Pomacentrus* and *Cheiloprion*. Only a few of these genera are covered here.

Amphiprion (clown fishes)

The most satisfactory of all for marine tanks. There are no unattractive species. In the wild these fishes rarely wander far from their host anemones and captivity is not a great burden to them provided that they have ample food and, of course, their beloved anemones. Although they may fight with one another (especially if there are more than two adult pairs in a medium-sized tank), they will not harm other fishes nor any other tank inhabitants.

Some of the larger species such as *A. ephippium* may bully smaller ones such as *A. percula,* particularly if anemones are scarce. Of the various species we have found *A. percula* to be the most timid with other clowns and they may sometimes have to be removed from a tank if the larger fish will not accept them. So far as feeding goes, clowns are very adaptable and readily, even greedily, accept most types of food.

A number of *Amphiprion* species have spawned in captivity, including *A. percula* and *A. ephippium,* but to date with only limited success in the rearing of the fry. All clowns become most pugnacious when breeding and are then particularly aggressive to others of their own kind (see section on Breeding).

Juvenile forms of Amphiprion

A. percula and *A. bicinctus* appear to breed true to type and the young from the smallest stage are miniature editions of the parent fish. We have not had an opportunity to study really juvenile forms of *A. perideraion* or *A. sebae,* but from half-grown specimens of these fishes which we have caught, we believe that there is no marked difference in colour between the young and the adults.

The fire clowns (*A. ephippium, frenatus* and *melanopus*) are a different story and appear to be just as confusing in the juvenile stage as when

85

adult. We have caught *Amphiprion* of the bright fire colour with two – or, more commonly, with three – white bands. All of these youngsters have lost the rear bands after a time, retaining only a single broad band over the gill cover. A faint black line remains for some time marking the site of the lost stripe(s). We have also frequently caught youngsters of the same size and colour in similar types of anemones and the same general surroundings, but without the additional bands. It seems, therefore, that some species may have additional stripes when very young, but we do not know which these are.

Amphiprion percula (common clown fish). Probably the most well known of any tropical marine fish. It has appeared on the postage stamps both of Singapore and of Australia. The brilliant orange and white bands with black edging seem almost to be painted on to the body, which rarely exceeds 3½ inches in length. Very hardy and the least pugnacious of the *Amphiprion* species, the popularity of this small clown is well deserved. It has a very distinctive, curtseying, almost tumbling motion which it can keep up for long periods, a characteristic which is not nearly so noticeable in the other species, especially the larger ones. This is the gayest and happiest of the whole family.

Amphiprion ephippium, frenatus, melanopus (Fire Clowns, Tomato Clowns). These three species are so similar as to be readily confused with each other, especially when not fully grown. There are minor differences, but some authorities have recently suggested that all three should be regarded as one species. *A. melanopus* differs from the others in having all black anal and ventral fins, whereas in *A. ephippium* and *A. frenatus* these fins are predominantly flame coloured. The young semi-adult body colour varies according to sex (and perhaps with locality and species also) from brilliant orange-red to a dark reddish-brown or near-black. When they reach full maturity all fire clowns have dark bodies and flaming pectoral, dorsal and caudal fins. The one broad band slashing the head and gill covers just behind the eyes is very distinctive. Basically it is white but can take on a bluish incandescence.

These fishes are larger than *A. percula* – we have seen them up to 6 inches long in the wild and they can probably grow larger. They are more pugnacious than many other clowns. Although widely distributed throughout the Indo-Pacific and very common in the reefs around Singapore, fire clowns are relatively uncommon in the clearer waters off Java and the east coast of Malaysia.

86

Because of their pugnacity it is rarely possible to keep more than one pair in any one tank. They may tolerate other species of *Amphiprion,* but even so, if the fire clowns are larger, they are best introduced concurrently with, or later than, the others. Care also has to be taken in introducing new males or females to a former solitary specimen. We have on many occasions had to stand by to prevent seemingly ideal partners from damaging or killing each other. It generally helps to introduce a larger female to a smaller male, rather than the other way around.

A well-settled pair of fire clowns is a joy. They are fearless in nature and rapidly become tame enough to accept food from their owner's fingers. They will bite at or nibble fingers trailed in the water and can inflict a sharp nip – not harmful or painful, but quite enough to be felt.

These fishes are particularly liable to catch *Oodinium* and, especially if just received from overseas, may need to be given a precautionary treatment with copper sulphate. (Check first with your supplier in case they have already had some such treatment.) They can also arrive with flesh wounds and fin damage, which if left could develop into fungus or tail and fin rot, both of which can prove fatal. Treatment for these troubles is described in the section on Diseases.

In the wild, fire clowns seem to prefer the beaded anemones which are most frequently found in crevices just below the low-water mark of the lowest spring tides. This is the area richest in corals, just where the fringing reefs plunge down to the deeper water. Because of their almost pathetic trust in the security provided by their anemones they are fairly easy to catch, especially as they are reluctant to leave home territory. When breeding they are particularly bold and fearless and we have been attacked on many occasions when swimming or wading too close to their breeding grounds.

These clowns can also be bred in captivity if one can secure a mated pair. It is worth going to some trouble to obtain such a pair, but due to their size at maturity they will need a larger tank than *A. percula.*

Amphiprion perideraion (Rose Clown). A truly beautiful little fish, not more than about 3½ inches long when fully grown. It is not aggressive except at breeding times and is one of our particular favourites. The body colour is a dusky rose with creamish white 'mane' running from head to tail along the back. In Malaysian specimens the fins are pearly white, but in those from Java they are tinged with gold, or all-gold. Both types are equally attractive and behave similarly.

A. perideraion is relatively hardy, but not quite so strong as *A. percula* and care should be taken to prevent bullying from larger fishes. It does not seem to be so prone to *Oodinium* as fire clowns and its general habits are very similar to those of *A. percula*.

We mostly find this fish in anemones of almost the same pink colour and it is extremely clever in eluding the net, using every inch of cover to the maximum. *A. perideraion* is usually found in large beds of these particular anemones and when chased will readily slip through the tentacles from one to another or even to another group some feet away. In this it is more enterprising than many other clowns which are prone to linger near their home anemones. This is the only one which we have found where a protective form of coloration seems to have developed to any extent. If the fish is put into a tank with anemones of various colours it will always select a pink one for its home. There is no record of *A. perideraion* being induced to spawn in captivity, although we had a pair which came very near to doing so.

Distribution of this species must be fairly wide and from our experience there can be colour variation of the fins. It is not found in the fringing reefs around Singapore and appears to prefer the clearer waters of the east coast of Malaysia and of Java. Although likely to be found over a wide area, this fish is never present in any great numbers and not easily caught. So far as we know, it is not yet exported commercially.

Amphiprion sebae (Black-and-White Banded Clown). In size this clown appears to be midway between *A. percula* and *A. ephippium*, i.e. about 4½ inches. It is slightly deeper and plumper in relation to its length. The clear-cut bands of bluish-white on the blackish-brown body and the well-coloured golden pectoral and caudal fins make this an attractive fish.

(There is another species – *A. xanthurus* – very close to this in appearance apart from the fact that its second white bar does not go right through to the outer margin of the dorsal fin and that it may have a third white bar on the caudal peduncle.)

A. sebae prefers deeper waters than *A. ephippium* or *A. percula* and is usually found from twenty to thirty feet down, but we have caught large specimens in relatively shallow water, in close proximity to the *Stoichactis* anemone. This leads us to think that it may come into shallower water to breed in these anemones.

This clown is usually much less aggressive than many of its cousins and makes a good community fish. In colour it is a good contrast to the other species.

A. sebae seems to be a little more delicate than others of the same

16. A 'waggle' *(Plectorhincus chaetodontoides)*
    Photograph by the author

17. An *Apogon nematopterus* with, in left hand corner, a species of *Euphyllia*
    and at right a young *Trachyphyllia geoffroyi* which grew its second 'head'
    in our tank

18. Small local fish, thought to be a species of *Apogon*, but known to us as a 'rainbow' fish, spotted scat (*Scatophagus argus*) and *Chaetodontoplus mesoleucus*. Both the latter fishes do well in a tank, but the rainbow fish does not and we have ceased to collect this species

19. Head of long-horned cow fish *(Lactoria cornuta)*
Photograph by the author

20. An attractive arrangement of pebbles, rocks and sand. The yellow coral is
a *Turbinaria* sp., beneath it appears a group of dormant *Tubastrea aurea*.
The pink and red branched growths are *Gorgonians*. (Note small goby on
stones)

21. A fine specimen of *Trachyphyllia geoffroyi*
   Photograph by the author

22. A coral of the *Euphyllia* genus, thought to be *Euphyllia fimbriata*. At left
   is part of a *Symphyllia* coral and in the background the daisy-like polyps
   of a *Goniopora*
   Photograph by the author

family and is usually the first to succumb to any outbreak of disease, sometimes with very little warning. We think that this may be due to the fact that it normally lives in deeper, cleaner waters where it is not subject to so many changes in temperature and salinity and is therefore less adaptable to tank conditions.

The fish has not yet been bred in captivity but as its habits and preferences seem to be similar to those of its fellows – apart from the liking for deep water – it should be possible to induce it to spawn. Provided, of course, that a mature pair can be found and acclimatized to the tank.

Like *A. perideraion*, it is more commonly found on the east coast of Malaysia and in Java than it is in Singapore.

Premnas biaculeatus (Maroon Clown). The colour is a glorious rich red which darkens with age, but still remains bright. The white bands are quite narrow; young specimens may have a third, on the caudal peduncle. In size this handsome fish is very similar to *A. ephippium* and can grow to about 6 inches. If anything, it is the more aggressive of the two and very given to fighting with its own kind. A maroon clown is well equipped for this with conspicuous spines in the pre-orbital region which are directed downwards. These can be a nuisance when removing such fish from a net. It is not aggressive towards other types of fish, excepting those small enough to be eaten without difficulty.

The behaviour is similar to that of *A. ephippium* and the fish is equally liable to contract *Oodinium,* fungus and tail and fin rot. If suitable precautions are taken, however, this clown should prove hardy and long-lived. We know of one which has been kept for at least seven years in the same tank and it has spawned regularly during that time. Its companion was five years old when it died, recently, and that was a replacement for the first mate which had died after two years in captivity.

This is a fish which will appeal to most people but it is not suitable for very small tanks nor for those containing delicate specimens. It needs a lot of room and will do best in an under-populated tank. It does not seem to be very widely distributed and we have only found it in Java.

Amphiprion (?) (Cardinal Clown). We do not know the specific name for this fish, a picture of which appears facing page 32.

Almost as large as *A. ephippium* – about 5 inches long – it is nevertheless a relatively peaceable member of the family and does not even bully other members of its own species very much. It is found under almost the same conditions as *A. bicinctus* and seems to be equally hardy.

89

Suitable precautions should, however, be taken against fungus and tail and fin rot. We have found this fish only in Java. One specimen which we had showed the remains of a juvenile line at the 'collar'.

This is a particular favourite of ours as it is the first clown fish which has bred in our tanks. The pair of fish in question were especially good-natured and did not resent our removing three ferocious *Cerianthus,* a number of corals and a large quantity of 'glass' shrimps and other potential enemies of the expected fry. They remained devoted parents throughout the hatching period. A description of the breeding procedure is given elsewhere in this book.

Dascyllus (various species)
Dascyllus have proved to be very satisfactory tank fishes; hardy and not quarrelsome. The only species which we have caught off Singapore is *D. trimaculatus. D. aruanas* appears to be the most widely distributed. Our *D. melanurus came from Indonesia.*

Dascyllus aruanas. This attractive small fish grows to 3–3½ inches. It is pearly white with three vertical blackish bars, the first through the eye, second through the dorsal spines down into the ventral fin and the third across the soft dorsal and into the base of the caudal peduncle. The rest of the tail and the tail fin is white.

Dascyllus melanurus. Similar to the foregoing species but with black tail fins. Very juvenile specimens are said to be entirely black but we have not had any so young. We kept two pairs of these in one of our outside tanks where they thrived and one of each pair regularly produced the black face which is the sign of breeding. (At such times the pearly white colour is liable to change to a cream tint or to take on a faintly yellowish look and the black part on the head looks fuzzy.) We cannot tell whether any of our own *D. melanurus* might have spawned because of the density of the corals and algae in the tank concerned, but their behaviour has been consistent with that of fishes guarding eggs. They could not hope to raise any fry, however, because of the presence of demoiselles and wrasses in the same tank. We know that *D. melanurus* have been bred in captivity in Djakarta.

Dascyllus trimaculatus. These fish attain 5½ inches in the wild but at this size their rich black colour has faded to a greyish, unattractive shade. They have a rounder body than other types of dascyllus, but this is not so obvious in the young, especially when the dorsal fins are erected; this makes them look almost triangular. In youth they are a deep velvety black with round white blotches on the nape and midway along the body on each side. There is also a black blotch at the base of the pectoral fin but this is not apparent in juveniles. The white spot on the nape disappears with age but the body spots may remain, and the colour deteriorates to greyish-brown. As we have noted in our section dealing with the relationship between clown fishes and anemones, *D. trimaculatus* also favours these creatures and will use them as a haven at night. We have not bred this fish, but if we wished to do so we would ensure that it was kept in a tank with anemones.

Abudefduf, Pomacentrus (Demoiselles or Damsel Fishes)
Most demoiselles (but not *Pomacentrus melanochir*) are quarrelsome and it is unwise to include more than two in any tank. We recommend the blue and the yellow ones only because small fishes of these colours are difficult to find. There is no point in using the dusky-black specimens as contrast fish as there are other dark coral fishes, notably *Dascyllus trimaculatus,* which are more attractive (at least when young) and less quarrelsome. Demoiselles do not grow beyond 4–6 inches and are easy to feed. They eat chopped shrimp readily but we have also seen them nibbling at algae. This is probably more in order to capture minute animals living upon it than to eat the algae. They dig small worms and other creatures out of the coral rock but we have not caught them eating coral.

Pomacentrus coeruleus (Blue Damsel Fish). This fish is also known as the blue devil. It has a blue body which looks darker on top than underneath. Some specimens may have a flushing of gold from the underlip along the underneath part of the body to the ventral fin. The head is marked with faint lines reminiscent of a horse's head-harness and across the forehead just above the eyes is a lighter blue band. A dark-blue spot appears at the back close to the soft-rayed dorsal and the fish has short dotted lines from the outer corner of each eye slanting upwards. When fully grown it has blue or bluish transparent fins. The best specimens come from Indonesia: local blue devils are smaller and darker.

   P. coeruleus will breed in captivity if kept under natural conditions without too much interference. It needs algae-covered glass or rock on which to spawn and does not clean the surface first as the clowns do.

Pomacentrus melanochir. This is similar to the above species but has a bright yellow tail. Ours have come from Indonesia. All have been very satisfactory and peaceable.

Abudefduf oxydon. There is another fish similar in shape to the blue devil which is not caught in Singapore, but which we have received from Indonesia. The body of the fish is blue-black which in some lights takes on a purplish bloom. It has a distinctive white band behind the pectoral fin bisecting the body. There are electric-blue, neon-bright markings: the first is a headband, but slanting slightly upwards, the second is parallel to this line and shorter; it passes from beneath the lower lip, under the eye to end just above the pectoral fin. Both stop short of the white band but are continued after an interval by two further lines also sweeping upwards. A third short line slants downwards from beneath the soft-rayed dorsal across the top of the caudal peduncle pointing in the direction of the head; it is parallel with the other two lines. Other fainter blue markings show on the head of the fish. Pectoral fins are colourless and all other fins blue-black. The specimens which we have had have been about 2 inches. These are lively, unusual-looking fish and in our opinion the best of all the small 'contrast' fishes. They are beautiful in their own right, apart from providing a foil for their companions.

Pomacentrus (?) (Yellow Demoiselle). This fish is comparatively rare locally and those which we have caught differ from the descriptions which we have of *Pomacentrus notophthalmus* and *Abudefduf aureus* sufficiently for us to believe that they are a different species. They are smaller and less quarrelsome than the blue devils.

Pomacanthidae

This family includes species with fantastically beautiful colours and markings, but some of them can grow to 15 inches which makes adult specimens rather unsuitable for a domestic tank. The only members of the family which we have seen in Singapore are *Pomacanthus semicirculatus* and *P. annularis*; both specimens had been trapped in wire cages and the latter was too badly damaged to survive. These fishes are not frequently caught in fishing nets, because they hide amongst the coral, and trapped specimens tend to get badly damaged by rubbing against the wire mesh in attempts to escape. We also suspect that they may fight with the other captives. The *P. semicirculatus* lived because it was trapped by a young boy who knew of our interest in fishes and who extricated it promptly and kept it safely until he could get a message to us that he had a 'pretty blue fish'. This fish was very timid at first and hid amongst the rocks for so long that we thought it must be dead. Then one day we saw a flash of blue, which was its tail, and gradually it became more confident until it was eating greedily of chopped shrimp. All Pomacanthidae are said to feed on invertebrates and vegetation from the rocks and we certainly noticed that a floating green 'blanket' seaweed which we put into the tank soon disappeared into the cave occupied by our *P. semicirculatus*. We have not seen this fish eat coral, but its mouth looks as if it could. The fish sleeps in a cave at night. At the 3- to 4-inch size it starts changing from its bright juvenile colour to the more sober markings of the adult. We believe that it can be kept successfully provided that it is not too large, nor at all damaged when caught. Single specimens do not fight with other tank inhabitants but are said to be quarrelsome with their own kind if any are added. Because of the eventual size of this fish we doubt whether breeding is practicable except possibly in a public aquarium. In fact, we cannot really recommend it to the private aquarist, nor, for that matter, would we suggest that *P. annularis* is any more suitable.

Family Chaetodontidae

Some of the most beautiful of the coral fishes belong to this family, which numbers 200 species but is not well represented in the waters around Singapore and Malaysia. We have caught only four species. All are quarrelsome with their own kind, especially if they are about the same size. Fortunately they do not mind being lone representatives of their species and since it seems that spawning is unlikely, there is no need to have more than one of each. (We think that they would not spawn without a plentiful supply of the corals which they like to eat, especially *Pocillopora damicornis*.) The only one of the few which we know that is not a coral eater is *Chelmon rostratus* and even that will sometimes nip the heads of tube worms. We do not know how widely spread the species are, but some with which we are familiar are found in the Philippines. If you are thinking of keeping any of the Chaetodontidae we suggest that you restrict your collection of live corals to those which they will be less liable to eat, such as *Alveopora excelsa, Fungia* (all species) *Goniopora* (all species) *Heliopora coerulea, Podabacia crustacea* and *Turbinaria* (all species).

Chaetodontoplus mesoleucus. A most attractive fish with violet blue lips, yellow face, broad black band through the eye, white forepart to body and black rear, having a blue margin to the soft-rayed dorsal and anal fins. There is a distinctive yellow smudge at the beginning of the anterior dorsal fin just behind the black band. The most noticeable feature is the bright pineapple-yellow tail which appears small in relation to the size of the fish and moves with a rather exaggerated action. We wondered why the distinctive violet-blue colour on the thick lips did not show in photographs, but on checking with some *Chaetodontoplus* in our tanks we discovered that this was because the fish had its mouth open most of the time. They have noticeably pink insides to their mouths and cruise around with them rather widely open so that even the teeth and inner mouth can be seen.

The fish frequents the coral reefs preferring the deeper water at the reef edge. It readily evades the net with a quick swish of its tail and can slip sideways under the coral ledges. Hand-caught specimens of 2 inches or more are hardy but fish which have been caught in wire mesh traps often have bad lacerations on the front part of the head and the snout from which they do not recover.

Chaetodon octofasciatus. This fish is similar in personality to that described above but the body is less oval and it only grows to about 5 inches. It is a greenish pale-yellow with eight vertical black stripes, the first passing through the eye and the last through the soft-rayed dorsal. Young specimens are most attractive, bright and active, but delicate. Older fish are quite hardy.

Chelmon rostratus. The butterfly fish of the Singapore stamp is one of the most spectacular of the reef fishes. It is very common in the Singapore area and is a frequent victim of the wire fishing traps because it cannot resist exploring any interesting-looking opening.

In appearance it is unmistakable with the long, pointed snout, deep pearly-grey body slashed with bold black-edged bars of deep golden-yellow, orange or apricot and a large black spot on the top of the last bar. It can grow to 9 inches in the wild.

On the reef it pecks a living from small worms, crabs or any other creatures of similar size but does not attack corals. It does, however, kill and eat small tube worms and will sometimes peck at and damage the larger ones. Clams with wide open gapes are particularly subject to attack by this fish, which will also kill other bivalves and eat the flesh.

Its beak-like snout is very well suited for the purpose. These considerations apart, it is a very satisfactory tank fish once it has settled down. Like many fishes caught fresh from the wild, it is intensely nervous at first and may not eat regularly for some time. This timidity can also extend to extreme pugnacity with others of its own species and if several freshly caught specimens are housed in one tank a careful watch should be kept to prevent undue bullying. We have known a number of smaller specimens to be killed by larger ones and even mature fish will sometimes die, apparently of shock, after fight injuries.

C. rostratus should always be treated gently as it is very much more nervous than most other fishes and is the only species which we have seen to die of fright. This happened to us when we were clearing a tank. The remaining fish, a butterfly, proved very active and eluded us until, when finally caught, he was dead – brilliant and in apparently perfect condition, but dead. Since then, we have made it a practice to remove these fish first of all before attempting any programme of reconstruction, so that they do not have time to become over-excited.

Any tank containing these fish should have at least one large cave and preferably a labyrinth beneath the mass of rockwork which forms the basis for the live corals. The butterfly fish will enjoy exploring all possible channels and openings, including some which you would not think it could possibly squeeze itself through. It has a way of slipping sideways – almost horizontally – through impossibly small gaps. When really domesticated it loses most of its natural nervousness and will take food from the hand. There is a very strong snapping movement of the jaws which can be heard at feeding time.

C. rostratus is a very inquisitive creature, always ready to investigate any new piece of rock or coral which is put into the tank. It is an excellent subject for photography and is usually in the forefront of the tank when pictures are being taken; it does not seem to be worried by flash.

Some reports say that this fish is liable to die if treated with copper sulphate, but we have not found this to be the case, nor do we find it very susceptible to diseases and parasites.

Parachaetodon ocellatus. This is another species found in Singapore, which we have sometimes bought from the fish market; it is similar to *C. rostratus* but is a caramel colour where that is yellow and has a short snout. *P. ocellatus* has never lived long in our tanks; this may have been due to the fact that it was not newly caught. It is an attractive fish but does not have the appealing air of the butterfly. Ours would eat well and appear to thrive, then just fade away.

Family Labridae – Wrasses

These are a world-wide family, embracing some of the most vivid creatures which live in the sea. Many of them are too large and active to confine in a home aquarium. No one who has seen *Thalassoma lunare* sweep in from deep water in flashes of iridescent blue-green fire will wish to cage it in a small space where the colours will fade and the fish droop until finally it dies, literally a pale shadow of its normal self.

Fortunately there are a number of very attractive dwarf wrasses which will live happily in captivity. Some of these are almost as brilliant as their larger relatives. Others, such as *Coris gaimard,* can be caught whilst still young when they make lovely small specimens.

Most wrasses which we have encountered have had the curious habit of sleeping under the sand. If no sand is present they will lie flat on the bottom as though dead. When wrasses are to be kept the tank should be provided with a relatively deep stretch of sand in which they can sleep. No fish will survive for long unless it feels reasonably secure in its surroundings; without security – even if it lives for a while – it will not show itself to best advantage. Wrasses need sand as much as clowns need anemones.

These are extremely active creatures and great hunters. Small fishes, crabs, worms and shrimps are all part of their normal fare. Even when amongst a rock network wrasses are very graceful swimmers and there is something snakelike in their posture when, with heads poised and bodies half coiled they pause before attacking their prey. Like *Chelmon rostratus,* wrasses are very inquisitive and like the demoiselles will often follow us about on the reef hoping, as the garden robin does, that we will turn up some small worms. They are also particularly fond of broken sea urchins.

Wrasses are not aggressive towards other types of fish but are sometimes vicious to those of their own genera. We have not seen them harm any corals nor the larger tube worms, but it is possible that they may attack smaller and more delicate tube worms which resemble their normal food. Nor have we seen them nibble at any algae: if they should do so we do not think that they will cause any serious damage.

Given a congenial environment, these fishes are very lively and attractive and the sight of a wrasse poking its head vertically through the sand

A species of Euphyllia – probably *Euphyllia fimbriata*.

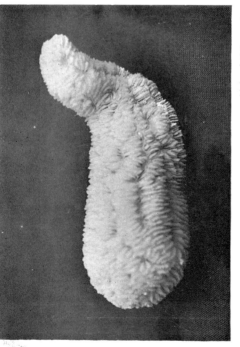

Two studies of *Polyphyllia talpina* the photograph bottom
Top: *Pectinia lactuca*. Bottom: *Herpolitha limax*.

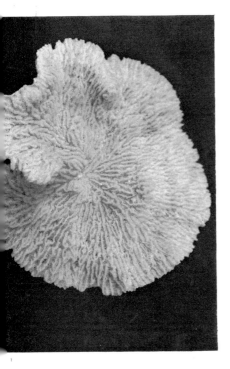

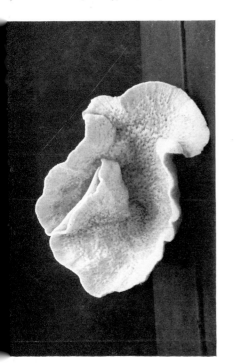

Top: Coral of the *Merulina* species – probably a young *M. ampliata* (not all of this species form frondlike projections). Bottom: *Fungia echinata*.

Two photographs of *Podabacia crustacea*. The bottom photograph shows clearly how a colony can form on the skeleton of the dead coral.

Top: *Oulastrea crispata* × 1.3. The slight enlargement allows the 'pattern' to show more clearly. Bottom: Coral of the genus *Acropora*: there are said to be 250 species of this coral in the Indo-Pacific and identification is difficult. None of the species which we have tried will live in our tanks.

Top: *Favia sp.* Bottom: An unidentified coral with a prettily marked skeleton, which also will not survive in captivity. We have not often found it in local waters.

Top: *Merulina ampliata.* Bottom: Crater-shaped coral, probably a *Turbinaria.*

Top: *Dendrophyllia nigrescens*. This coral will not live for long

Top: *Favites abdita*. Bottom: *Goniopora* sp.

Top: *Platygyra lamellina*. Bottom: *Platygyra lamellina* a closer view.

Top: *Goniastrea sp.* Bottom: *Lobophyllia hemprichii.*

to look around before launching itself into a new day never loses its charm. The going-to-bed performance is just as fascinating: with a squiggle and a flurry of sand it is bedded down for the night and we sometimes find it very difficult to detect where exactly a fish is lying buried.

Coris gaimard. These fish are said to attain 12 inches but the specimens which we have had have been of the 3 to 3½ inches size and our description refers to them at this stage: the markings get duller as they grow older, although the blue freckles and yellow caudal fin remain. The species is widely distributed in the Indo-Pacific although we have not found them in the reefs off Singapore. They prefer the deep waters of a lagoon to the intertidal zone of the reefs and ours have come from Indonesia. The body of the fish is red, deepening to brown nearer to the caudal peduncle and the back part is heavily freckled with iridescent royal-blue spots which become sparser towards the front of the body. There are five distinctive white bars all outlined in black or very dark-brown. One runs down the snout. The first of the others, which are all vertical, comes from the top of the head just behind the eye. The second runs from the first dorsal fin ending behind the pectoral fin; this is the longest. The third is approximately midway between the second and the fourth which comes from just behind the soft-rayed dorsal. These bars are all untidy in outline and might almost be described as blotches. The dorsal fins are bright-red but in some specimens the white bars may extend through the fin. The anal fins are red with a blue outer margin and a distinct inner blue line running parallel to it. The caudal fin is golden-yellow and it is bounded successively by red, black, and blue vertical lines on the caudal peduncle, the line nearest to the head being red. The ventral fins are red and the pectoral fins transparent-yellowish. *C. gaimard* has been described as a lazy fish but we have found that it is very busy in a tank which has rocks – always pecking about for small worms. It sleeps under the sand.

Cleaner Wrasses. We have kept only one species of cleaner wrasse in our tanks – *Labroides dimidiatus.* These are fascinating creatures and will immediately set up cleaning stations as soon as they are introduced to a tank. They do this by spiralling up and down showing themselves to attract customers. At first the other occupants are liable to be suspicious of the cleaners and may try to fight them off – there is a common green wrasse which we find in waters around Singapore which has been known to kill them, and clown fishes and Malayan angels are particularly suspicious of their intentions. Rabbit fishes, on the other hand, seem to welcome them and once they have some customers others will follow. There is a danger in this if you have any very predatory fishes in your tank – we had a frog fish which would position itself where it could make a grab at the smaller customers and which had to be returned to the sea. Another danger is that you may introduce into your tank a bogus cleaner such as *Aspidontus rhinorhynchus* which is not a wrasse but a member of the blenny family masquerading as a cleaner in order to take a nip at the other fishes. There are some grounds for suspicion that cleaner wrasses may occasionally damage coral or be too rough with their clients and they should be watched for these faults. They are delicate and difficult to keep unless you have a good number of fishes for them to clean, but they do not depend exclusively upon their customers for food – they will eat chopped shrimp greedily.

Labroides dimidiatus (Blue-and-White Cleaner). The specimens which we have had have been about 3 inches and have come from Indonesia. A similar wrasse is found in Hawaii and we believe that the species may be widely distributed although we do not get them in the waters around Singapore. The front part of the body is white and the back part pale-blue. There is a blue-black line starting from the snout and passing through the eye, broadening towards the tail. This goes right through the caudal fin. Another dark line goes across the top of the head and down the centre of the back stopping at the end of the soft-rayed dorsal. (This line shows only faintly when the fish is seen side-view, but is clearly visible if you are looking at it from above.) There is a similar line beneath the fish but starting farther back near the ventral fins and continuing into the caudal fin where it may merge with the broad central line. Dorsal, anal and ventral fins are pale-blue; pectorals transparent, apparently colourless. We had one of these fish which would always try to clean our arms if we reached down into the tank. Although amusing and graceful to watch we cannot recommend the cleaner wrasses because they are delicate.

Brown-and-White Striped Wrasse (Believed to be Coris julis). We have only had one specimen, which came from Indonesia, where the species is common. Ours was about 2½ inches and the body was marked with very distinct stripes. A central very dark-brown or blackish stripe passes from the snout through to the caudal peduncle ending at the caudal fin which is pale gold. Above and below this dark stripe are two white ones (one above, one below) which each gives place to a lighter-brown stripe following the contours of the body. The top brown stripe ends in a white line along the top of the head and back and the lower one merges with white on the underside of the body. All the fins are white except for the caudal fin. This is not a dull-looking fish; the white throws the brown into relief and the stripes are well defined. Although similar to the cleaners in shape, this fish will not clean.

Grey-Hooded Wrasse. We have had several of these fish, some caught in Singapore and some in Indonesia. Those which we have had from Singapore have been paler in colour but the markings have been the same. All our specimens have been about 2 inches long. The head looks like a grey hood, sometimes with darker colour on the top and this hood ends in a white band behind the pectoral fin. The back part of the fish is black but the caudal peduncle and caudal fin are gold. Dorsal and anal fins are blackish, ventral fins white or pale-grey and pectoral fins white. The fish can attain 12 inches in the wild. The juvenile form of this fish has a brownish-gold coloured body with black markings. It does not completely change over to the adult colour until it reaches about 2 inches.

Golden Wrasse. The specimens which we have had have come from Indonesia and have not exceeded 3 to 4 inches in size. The fish probably grows at least another 2 inches in the wild and may undergo some colour change whilst doing so. There is the possibility that our specimens have been young *Thalassoma lutescens* (the yellow wrasse) in which case they would eventually reach 8 inches and the head must later become grey or bluish with broken greenish or brown bands and the body colour might become duller. The anal and dorsal fins would develop grey-blue bands. We think, however, that our golden wrasse is a separate species.

It is a clear golden colour all over, smaller specimens being rather lemon-gold. The dorsal fins are clear with a faintly greenish tinge but at the 4-inch size may develop a trace of blue horizontal bands. Young specimens have a faint black dot at the beginning of the dorsal fin followed by two more evenly spaced black dots outlined in white, and a clear black dot on the caudal fin. Older specimens have a clearer black dot at the beginning of the dorsal fin but lose the white circle around the middle dot and the third dot becomes very faint; there is only a trace of the dot on the caudal fin. This fin has a reddish tinge in young fish and the red colour intensifies as they get older.

There is a distinctive post-ocular scale which is not greatly different from the body colour in young specimens but becomes greenish as they get larger. Older fish have traces of horizontal green and red lines on the gill covers.

The behaviour is typically wrasse-like. Once established the fish is satisfactory in the tank, adds a welcome streak of gold, and feeds readily of chopped shrimp and small creatures pecked out of the rocks.

Lepidoplois mesothorax (Harlequin Fish). The front half of the body is purplish-grey, darkening towards the rear, this dark colour ending in a clearly defined diagonal slanting from the soft-rayed dorsal back towards the front of the body to terminate at a point behind the pectoral fin. From this diagonal the back part of the body is yellow with faint pink flushing and so also is the caudal peduncle and caudal fin. The soft-rayed dorsal and anal and ventral fins are bright yellow and the pectoral fin is paler yellow. The dorsal fins are dark. There is a dark line passing from the mouth to a black spot at the base of the pectoral fin where there is also a bright golden spot which flashes with the movements of the fish. We have seen this fish pecking amongst the tentacles of an anemone.

Bird Wrasses. These belong to the genus *Gomphosus* and have long beak-like snouts, which are used for pecking about amongst the coral. We had two small ones about 3 to 4 inches in length respectively which were an attractive brown colour with lighter undersides. The smaller – about 3 inches long – was a particularly handsome golden-brown, darker markings on the head and snout emphasizing the beak-like effect. Some experts believe that these little brown fishes are females, the males being a green colour. Large specimens may reach 10 inches, but the smaller ones make very good tank fish, being hardy once established. They are very interesting to watch with their bird-like movements.

Acanthuridae. The surgeon fishes belong to this family. They get their common name from the extremely sharp spines which most of them carry on the caudal peduncle. Most have other, poisoned, spines amongst the various fins, although the distribution of these spines varies according to the species. Those belonging to the genus *Naso* frequently have bumps or horny protuberances on the forehead.

Surgeon fishes can be very attractive and we have had specimens with pale, nearly opalescent, colouring. One of the most beautiful is *Paracanthurus theuthis*, with its purplish-blue body marked with black and its

100

golden tail. However, our experience with surgeon fishes is relatively limited. Small specimens are very delicate, but once they grow above the 2 to 3 inches size they appear to be reasonably robust. Nevertheless, surgeon fishes are not the easiest of specimens to adapt to aquarium life and newcomers to marine fish-keeping are advised to avoid this genus at least until they have gained more experience.

These fishes appear to live mostly on algae and are difficult to feed whilst in captivity. They will not readily take chopped shrimp at feeding time, although it is possible that they may pick up scraps from the rocks later.

Family Diploprionidae

The only member of this family found locally which is suitable for the fish tank is *Plectorhincus chaetodonoides*.

Plectorhincus chaetodonoides. This fish is one of our favourites. The body is brown with large white spots which have smaller brown ones inside them and the fins are brown and white except for the ventral fin which, in our specimens, has been all-brown. In the wild *P. chaetodonoides* can grow to 12 inches in length but many smaller specimens can be found and we have had them of all sizes from just over 1 inch to about 8 inches. Tank life will stunt full growth. This fish is very satisfactory in the larger communal tank because it is one of the most peaceable of reef fishes despite the apparently large mouth. In fact the mouth is not very big, but the exceptionally thick lips give this appearance. A largish specimen is usually included as 'boss fish' in our bigger tanks and we have yet to find any case of bullying – even of newly introduced fishes.

This fish seems rarely, if ever, to sleep. If it does so, it must sleep whilst in motion. Even at 3 a.m. we have found one of these still patrolling the tank. Smaller specimens swim with a very much exaggerated undulating action; our pet name for them is 'waggle fish'. On the reef they are particularly difficult to catch amongst the craggy coral, swimming serenely on, just a few inches from the edge of the net, and giving an occasional little extra skip or wriggle to avoid capture.

Possibilities of breeding this attractive fish are not great, as breeding size would be much larger than that which can be accommodated in a normal tank. The fish is also a roamer: we have always found solitary specimens. This means that tank conditions are unlikely to approach those in which it would naturally breed.

101

Family Apogonidae (Cardinal Fishes)

The family is said to be represented, in Malaysian and Singapore waters, by about thirty species, of which the most colourful that we have seen is *Apogon nematopterus*.

Apogon nematopterus. A hardy and attractive little fish. The largest specimens we have had have been 3 to 4 inches when adult, but we believe that the fish can grow larger in the wild. The red eye and lemon-tinted ventral fins, together with the pattern of reddish spots on the rear of the body, behind a broad central vertical black line, gives the species a distinctive appearance. The colours are naturally brighter in the smaller specimens, but even the adults are very attractive.

The fish is a hoverer, both in the wild and in the tank, but is rarely to be found far from cover. On the reef it is often surprised amid the branches of coral such as *Hydnophora rigida* and appears to be almost stationary. On the approach of a collecting net it vanishes quietly and without any impression of haste, but very effectively. Its weak point is the fact that it is very loyal to one area and is always reluctant to vacate its chosen pitch.

A. nematopterus may be semi-nocturnal in its hunting habits and it certainly has very large eyes suited to this type of work. We have noticed at night, when shining a torch into the tank, that these fish are still hanging in mid-water and very rapidly move into the beam of the torch, snapping at plankton. Possibly they hunt similarly in bright moonlight or at morning or evening, when a great deal of minute life that will not venture abroad in full daylight comes into the open water.

We suspect that other fishes of this Apogonidae family such as the cardinal fish – *Amia brachygramma* – are essentially nocturnal in their hunting. We have never caught them free-swimming during the day and only find them when lifting large pieces of coral such as *Hydnophora rigida* or *Acropora hyacinthus*. They will hide within the branches of such corals in much the same way as some members of the Gobiidae family.

A. nematopterus are very satisfactory and peaceable in the tank; they seem to prefer to cruise around together. Although we have not heard of them being bred in captivity we think that this should be possible, provided a pair can be found and persuaded to settle.

Family Monacanthidae (Leather Jackets, Trigger Fish, File Fish)
These are very common fishes. The family is not generally so colourful as the better known Balistidae, which are not well-represented in Singapore and Malaysian waters. There are eight species of Monacanthidae known locally and they are mostly brownish or greenish.

These fishes are weak swimmers and they are mostly found amongst weeds or on the reefs. All have the ability to vary their colouring dramatically so as to fade into the background and most will change colour as they move from one part of the tank to another. They prefer not to swim in the open but tend to lurk in the shadows. Monacanthidae are said to scrape their food from the rocks and coral, presumably using the long first dorsal spine for the purpose. In the tank they settle down to eating chopped shrimp with an occasional nibble at seaweed. Most species are hardy but *Oxymonacanthus longirostris* is more delicate.

Oxymonacanthus longirostris. This is a file fish which we have received from Indonesia. When it is awake the colours are spectacular. The body length when full-grown is 2 to 3 inches. The basic body colour is turquoise with seven rows of irregular orange-yellow dashes and dots running horizontally. The fins appear to be clear, almost colourless, but there is an irregular black mark on the caudal fin and that fin has a trace of the body colour extending into it. The long snout is orange-yellow with horizontal lines of the same colour extending from it, the top one ending beneath the base of the file. The eye has a dark pupil with light turquoise and orange-yellow markings on the iris.

The anal and dorsal fins extend to the base of the caudal peduncle in a long unbroken line and provide the motive power, the fish moving the rear fins more vigorously than those nearer the front and thus pushing itself through the water. The caudal fin is not used for propulsion and is not fully spread when the fish is swimming. The swimming angle of the body is with head inclined downwards at 25 to 40 degrees and the fish has difficulty in picking up food from the surface of the water. Its food is slow-moving live food – not too large, because the mouth is small.

At night *O. longirostris* sleeps in crevices of *Acropora,* the file acting almost like a spring catch to hold it in position. When the fish is asleep the body colours fade and irregular dark blotches appear at intervals on the body.

Stephanolepis auratus is the trigger fish with which we are most familiar.

103

Stephanolepis auratus. This species has a rough, leathery skin which is mottled in greenish-grey with darker markings. The mouth is snout-like and the first dorsal spine is long and strong. It can be locked upright by a small weak second dorsal spine immediately behind it. These fish can grow quite large in the wild, but the biggest which we have had was about 2 inches. Because of their habit of nipping the heads off tube worms and sometimes snapping at the fins of other fishes we cannot recommend them as tank fish, but they are amusing and very hardy.

Family Monodactylidae (Silver Batfish)

There are two species occurring in Singapore and Malaysian waters, of which the most frequently caught, and the one which we know, is *Monodactylus argenteus* – commonly known as the silver batfish, moonfish or Malayan angel fish. By the latter name it will be familiar to freshwater aquarists. The Monodactylidae frequent coastal waters, trawling grounds and estuaries and are sometimes also found in freshwater. They are regarded as a food fish in Malaysia and normally swim in shoals.

Monodactylus argenteus. This has a deep, almost round, compressed body, silvery in colour but the young have two long narrow vertical lines on each side, one passing through the eye and the other through the back of the pectoral fin. The dorsal and ventral fins are gold and the tail fin a paler yellow. This species can grow to 9 inches in the wild. The mouth is small with feeble teeth.

These fish are an attractive addition to the tank; peaceable and quick moving, they cruise around in a rough formation and love to nibble at seaweed, especially the type like fine grass which we call 'blanket weed'. They also eat chopped shrimp, indeed we believe that they are mainly carnivorous. They have sometimes been seen attempting to remove parasites from a *Chelmon rostratus*. Like the scats, which are also better known as freshwater fish, Malayan angels really thrive best in salt water and we have had no trouble with them damaging themselves on the sharp corals, even though they are not strictly reef fish.

Family Ostraciontidae (Boxfish, Cowfish)

This is a most fascinating family, all of which have a boxlike armour of hexagonal bony scales. Some species have one or two hornlike projections in the front of the head. It is with the long-horned cowfish that we are familiar.

Lactoria cornuta (Long-horned Cowfish). The textbook says 'A pair of slender, elongate, antorbital spines directed forwards. Each ventral ridge ending in a similar long slender spine directed backwards. Caudal very elongate in adults.' A young Chinese friend describes it more vividly: 'That fish looks like cow, grunts like pig, swims like helicopter.' *L. cornuta*, at least when young, is yellow with Cambridge-blue markings on the scales. We had one specimen which was only about 3 inches long and very friendly. He would take food from our fingers and swim to the top of the tank to 'butt' at our hands. Boxfish are supposed to be poor swimmers, but can be fast-moving in the tank. We did not notice our small one grunting, but a larger specimen made a terrible noise. The latter was put back into the sea because he was 12 inches long and seemed to be cramped. Our specimens ate readily of chopped shrimp and would nose around in the seaweed. This might have been merely out of curiosity or in the hope of finding small parasites: we have not seen them eat it. We have, however, seen them mouthing algae on the side of the tank. Apart from reservations about their hardiness we would recommend small specimens because they are most attractive and amusing and do no harm.

Family Platacidae (Batfish)

The only species which we have found is *Platax teira*. When young it has noticeably long dorsal and anal fins but the body fills out in the older specimens to make the lengths of these appear less disproportionate. Juveniles are brownish-orange with pale-orange or pale-yellow crossbars, one through the eye, one through the pectoral fin and one through the soft dorsal and anal fins. Young specimens also have a light margin to the dorsal and anal fins and a light-coloured caudal fin. These bright colours gradually darken and by the time the fish have achieved a depth from tip of dorsal fin to tip of anal fin of about 6 inches they are predominantly dark-brown with three slightly lighter crossbars. Young specimens are found floating in seaweed close to the shore and if disturbed will fall down through the water like a sycamore seed.

P. teira is delicate when young but becomes hardy as it grows older, and very tame. They will take chopped shrimp from the hand. We have also seen one nibbling at seaweed, but this may have been to get at some hydroids enmeshed in it. Because they grow rapidly in the tank and ultimately, in the wild at least, attain 20 inches, they are not very suitable tank fish except for a large aquarium. Moreover, they seem to attract parasites, which may not harm the fish but spoil its appearance.

If the parasites are dispersed by treatment the fish soon becomes re-infested.

Family Scatophagidae (Scats)

The family is well distributed throughout the Indo-Pacific but there is only one common local species.

Scatophagus argus (Spotted Scat or Butterfish). This is the scat found in Singapore and Malaysian waters. It is a pale yellowish-green or greenish-grey or olive colour, lightening to silver, with large dark spots and an almost velvety bloom. The young have tawny markings on the forehead. The fins are equipped with long rigid spines, sometimes said to be poisonous. (As the fish are frequently found in dirty waters we think that any poisoning following a prick may be due to the water rather than to venom.) Adults can attain 12 inches but even very small specimens are hardy and disease resistant. These fish are at home in the sea, in estuaries and in rivers, but retain their colour best and seem healthier if kept in salt or brackish water. All of the specimens which we have had have been taken from the sea and kept in saltwater.

Scatophagus argus has been exported to temperate climates for many years as a freshwater fish. It is an excellent tank specimen as a general rule, although we have had one outbreak of fin-nibbling. This may have been because the tank in question had a high proportion of parasites and the scats were intending to attack these rather than their hosts. Scats love to nibble at the 'blanket' seaweed which we put into the tank but the main part of their diet is chopped shrimp.

Family Siganoidea (Rabbit Fish)

There are several members of this family which are commonly found around Singapore and in Malaysian waters. All, when young, are silvery with white, pale-blue, grey or bronze freckles or blotches. In some species these may coalesce into bars or wavy lines. The fishes have a distinctive oval shape, attractive sapphire-coloured eyes and a profile which is noticeably rabbit-like. So also is their nibbling action. They mostly swim together, the different species mixing easily, and if they come across a piece of seaweed they will not rest until they have eaten the whole of it. We have to keep a special tank of 'blanket' seaweed for them and we pull off pieces when required. These fishes will also eat algae from the glass of the tank and they like chopped raw shrimp. They may be vegetarian when young, but at about the three-quarter-inch size they will eat shrimp. Local fishermen claim that they can be caught in traps baited with pineapple, bananas or even rice. The dorsal, anal and ventral fins are well armed with sharp spines containing poison which can inflict a painful stab. These spines flick up and down with the movement of the fins with almost mechanical precision – rather like the opening and shutting of a fan. Adults may attain 11 to 20 inches according to species, but our experience is of the ¾ to 3 inch size. Such specimens are satisfactory in a tank: not quarrelsome, amusing to watch, very active and hardy. When older these fish are masters of camouflage and some seem able to suffuse themselves with yellow when against a light background.

Two of the most easily recognized species are *Siganus virgatus* and *Siganus guttatus*. The former has two dark bars – one from the chin through the eye to the beginning of the dorsal fin and the other parallel with it, curving up from the base of the pectoral fin. The pale spots of this species are rather indistinct. The latter does not have the dark bands and has small leopard-like bronze coloured markings. The young sometimes develop a distinctive yellow blotch beneath the soft-rayed dorsal fin which is most attractive. Both species have blue markings on the face.

Family Gobiidae (Gobies, Gobiodon)
This is a very extensive family and there are many species found locally. Some of these little fishes are very delicately marked and they are all a useful addition to the tank, because they are active at the bottom and eat fragments of food left there. Not that they are backward in coming to the upper levels at feeding time, to seize surprisingly large pieces of chopped raw shrimp. They will also suck sand from the bottom, dribbling it back when they have extracted nourishment from it. Several thousand young gobies have hatched in our tanks, but we doubt whether any have survived to the adult stage. Nor can we usually tell which are the parents – we may see several females ready to spawn, but then the next thing we notice are the masses of little silvery fry at the top of the tank.

Some species of *Gobiodon* are very attractive. They rarely exceed 1 inch in length. Specific identification is extremely difficult but we have found three distinct types in our area and there must be more. Our favourite is a bright-green or bluish-green with red markings, which we think is *G. rivulatus*, but we have also found others which are the smoky-grey colour of Persian cats and yet others which are black. We have only found these little fishes within the branches of *Acropora* corals. It is

107

possible that like the cardinals they are night hunters or, being so small in size, they may not need any more food than that which comes to them within the safety of the coral. No species of *Acropora* will live in our tanks. These fish seem to be immune to the nematocysts of other corals, however, and we have noticed them lying for long periods on some species of *Goniopora* and *Fungia* and on *Trachyphyllia geoffroyi*. On one occasion we saw a *Gobiodon* lying on a rather small pink sand anemone and it emerged unscathed, later to roost under the tentacles of the same anemone. In the security of tank life these are quite bold little fish and will come into mid-water to secure their food. They are hardy once established but until it proves possible to domesticate *Acropora* corals we do not think that they will be bred in captivity.

None of the Gobiidae family which we have kept have harmed corals, seaweeds nor any other tank creatures.

Family Trypauchenidae (Burrowing Gobies)

These fishes live in burrows in the mud or sand and are particularly common on sand bars and coral-reef flats. Specific identification is difficult. They often make their homes in the burrows of pistol prawns. (These prawns are very common members of the family Synalpheidae and are found in the intertidal zones. Despite this they do well at the bottom of the marine tank – see section on Crustaceans.)

Burrowing gobies will seek out any such prawn in the tank and occupy its burrow without apparent resentment on the part of the prawn, although it is doubtful whether the gobies render any service to the hosts. At the slightest suspicion of danger they back into their holes. They can get in head first, but nearly always prefer to keep their heads facing the danger. A favourite game of the children on the sandbars is to tease the gobies back into the holes by swimming over them in shallow water. Another is to trickle sand into the hole and watch the prawn shovelling it out again. The feeding habits of burrowing gobies are similar to those of the Gobiidae, but they are more reluctant to come to the top part of the tank to get food.

Family Centriscidae (Razor Fishes)

There are several members of this family found locally. They have long, thin, flat bodies, generally silvery with a dark lateral line. The shape is rather like that of the old-fashioned 'cut-throat' razor and the fishes swim in shoals with tails downwards and heads inclined towards the

108

surface. They are often found amongst weed beds and are slow moving. The size is about 6 inches at maturity but very small specimens are sometimes found. Because of their inability to compete for food against faster swimmers we do not recommend these, nor the Syngnathidae family, for a community tank.

Family Syngnathidae (Pipe Fishes, Sea Horses)

Pipe fishes are thin, tube-like and usually have long snouts. Their overall length does not exceed 6 to 7 inches. The eggs are often attached to the belly of the male which sometimes has a special brood pouch. These fishes are usually dull-coloured and not very attractive. They swim amongst weeds and some species will tolerate brackish water.

Sea horses are too well known to need description: usually they are dull-coloured although yellow ones can be found. In the wild their size can reach 12 inches but when found they are often smaller. It is sometimes possible to catch a male with eggs in the pouch and these can be detected by the swelling in the ventral area. The young will emerge in due course into the tank but they are most difficult to keep and we have never succeeded in rearing any to maturity.

8. Breeding and Spawning of Fishes

This chapter does not cover the raising of young marine fry to maturity because we have not yet progressed so far. We have been fortunate, however, in having a number of spawnings of various fishes. The circumstances of *Amphiprion* spawnings in our tanks are described in some detail to give an indication of the conditions in which such fishes can be induced to breed.

We are particularly indebted to Dr Lev Fishelson of Tel-Aviv University for permission to report some of his observations on the group spawning of *Dascyllus aruanas* and the successful spawning and rearing of a Mediterranean blenny – *Blennius pavo*.

Our thanks are also due to Mr Lee Chin Eng of Djakarta for permission to include data collected by him concerning some of the numerous spawnings which have taken place in his aquarium.

General observations

Reef-dwelling fishes appear to be remarkably consistent in their breeding procedures. Naturally there are differences in habits but in essentials they are very much the same.

Experience to date indicates that the Pomacentridae family, including all species of *Amphiprion* and *Dascyllus*, give a marked degree of parental care and attention to the eggs until they are actually hatched. (So do many other reef creatures such as the various species of cowries. Indeed, none of the relatively limited number of eggs would be likely to survive if unguarded in the dangerous waters of the reef.) In our experience all the eggs hatch out during the night – the heaviest incidence (at least with *Amphiprion*) being in the very early hours of the morning until just before dawn. Eggs unhatched during the first night do not appear to hatch until the next evening. Presumably the few hours of darkness allow the emergent fry time to gather strength before the majority of predators wake to active life. This night hatching experience is confirmed by Mr Lee Chin

110

Eng who has had repeated spawnings of Pomacentridae over the past eight years. Dr Fishelson's experience with *Dascyllus* differs in that his fish spawned either in the early morning or in the late afternoon and the fry hatched out 51 hours later, apparently irrespective of the amount of daylight available.

Most species of *Amphiprion* will lay their eggs in close proximity to an anemone. Although anemones provide some degree of protection we do not think that they play any other part in the hatching procedure. We have, however, noticed the fish fluffing the tentacles over the eggs as though perhaps to impregnate or coat them. We have also noticed that immediately prior to hatching the parents seem to force the anemone back from the eggs. In one instance the mating procedure of *A. perideraion* appeared to be stimulated by a milk-like substance emitted from the central cavity of a *Radianthus* anemone which fluid was eagerly gobbled up by the fish.

In all the cases which we have observed, *Amphiprion* appear to clean the rocks before laying – for some reason which we do not understand they also clear pits in the sand at the foot of the rock. Both parents guard and fan the eggs for the whole period of hatching.

According to Mr Lee Chin Eng, *Dascyllus* do not in his experience clean the rocks but if spawning on algae-covered glass will interrupt their laying so as to avoid any recently cleaned sections. But Dr Fishelson states categorically that 'Spawn places of *Dascyllus* . . . are in all cases clean surfaces, that are in nature normally cleaned by the fish itself'.

So far as *Amphiprion* are concerned the only spawnings of which we know have been with mated pairs. *Dascyllus aruanas* on the other hand, will either breed in pairs or indulge in group spawnings, as many freshwater fishes do. Another difference is that of the latter only the males guard and tend the eggs; the females taking no interest in the matter. A particularly vivid account of the group spawning of *D. aruanas* is given by Dr Lev Fishelson in the *Bulletin of the Sea Fish Research Station, Haifa* (No. 37), dated June 1964. In the case of the fish which he was observing, spawning took place in the summertime, i.e. June to August, in Israel.

Gobies lay their eggs in holes or even in the rocks and usually the first sign of breeding is clouds of fry drifting to the surface. We have not yet succeeded in raising the fry to maturity. Blennies appear to breed similarly, the young fry not descending to the bottom of the tank until they are 27 days old. According to Dr Fishelson's account, given in the *Israel Journal of Zoology*, Volume 12, Nos 1–4, December 1963:

'The females, attracted to the male by his courting behaviour, spawn on the walls of the latter's nesting hole. The spawn is protected and aerated by the male who drives the females away . . .

The number of eggs spawned by 2 to 3 females in the nest of a single male varies from 800 to 1200. . . .

The first larvae hatch 225 to 235 hours after spawning. . . .'

Temperature and pH

Dr Fishelson reports that his *Dascyllus* spawned at a water temperature of 25 degrees Centigrade (77 Fahrenheit) and a *pH* of 7·4 and the blennies at a temperature of about 24 degrees Centigrade (75·2 Fahrenheit) and a *pH* of 7·4–7·6. We have never measured the *pH* of our tanks, but the water temperature at the time of spawning was 78 to 80 degrees Fahrenheit.

The breeding of sea horses with the embryo fostered in the brood pouch of the male has been fully described in many books. We have often had these fascinating small creatures emerging in our tanks – they usually leave the pouch hooked together by their 'tails' and have to struggle to free themselves, which they do by remarkably strong kicking movements. Unfortunately we have never succeeded in keeping them for more than two or three days.

As a general rule we do not think that marine fishes will reproduce in completely sterile tanks. To the best of our knowledge breeding has only been observed in aquaria receiving frequent changes of seawater or under natural system conditions.

The spawning of Amphiprion observed in our own tanks

Local clown fishes are reputed to spawn mainly between November and March, a time coinciding roughly with the north-east monsoon, the onset of which varies somewhat in different parts of South East Asia. During the monsoon period plankton in the sea becomes more plentiful and the opacity of the water increases. The impulse to spawn at this time may therefore be a provision of nature designed to ensure for the young fry a plentiful supply of food and maximum protection from predators. Even so, it is probable that circumstances of captivity may affect the time of spawning and that this may also vary between the species.

Our first detailed observation of spawning behaviour was of two little *A. perideraion* which had settled in adjacent pink anemones in the front of a large tank. These anemones formed part of a chain of three pink ones and one purple. The latter had recently been added to the tank. The prospective parents had chosen the two largest of the pink anemones, the female occupying that next to the new purple one. There were many other fishes, corals, etc., in the tank, which had sand at the bottom.

A certain amount of mating behaviour had occurred between the two rose clowns and one evening we noticed that the larger one – presumably the female – looked broody. Her eyes were bright and clear and her creamy dorsal fins glistening but she was lying on her anemone as if enjoying a feeling of lassitude.

Presently the smaller fish began butting at the centre of the purple anemone, which then gave off a milky, dense substance. He gobbled up this fluid and it seemed greatly to excite him. The female, and all the other fishes, became interested and the tank flourished as it does when corals or tube worms are breeding. The anemone continued to emit the substance occasionally throughout the evening and the love play between the two *A. perideraion* increased. In the morning the anemones were flourishing and the pair were still interested in each other, but they had not spawned. The female again looked broody and was lying lazily against the tentacles of her anemone, so that when it flexed itself into the 'closing' position she went for a ride tail first towards the central cavity. We were afraid that she would be swallowed.

In the evening the clowns recommenced spawning behaviour and towards midnight one of them became very fierce, warning off others of the same type with a clucking coo which could be heard from the other side of a large room, and attacking them and then returning to one or other of the two anemones occupied by itself and its mate. Both partners were now using each other's anemones indiscriminately and sometimes sharing the same one. They would lie alongside each other, briefly, wriggling through the tentacles together or momentarily one would lie across the other. They cleaned the rock beneath both anemones, spitting out the sand. The male grew more and more excited and started butting the female. Some time after midnight we turned out the lights and went to bed in the hope that the clowns would spawn in the darkness. They still had not done so by morning, however, and shortly after this we discovered that the tank was being poisoned by the putty which had been used to set the glass. It had to be dismantled and the clowns lost their spawning impulse. Nevertheless, we are convinced that they came very close to spawning on this occasion.

The second time when we watched mating behaviour between two of our clowns we were more fortunate – this time they spawned.

We had received a pair of cardinal clowns from Mr Lee Chin Eng of Djakarta. On arrival they were put into a tank 36 × 16 × 22 inches together with two large *Cerianthus*, one large and several small anemones, a small amount of live coral and a good deal of coral rock, crabs, small 'glass' shrimps, blue sponge and two small *Astrophyton* living in a piece of nearly dead *Gorgonia*. Because of shortage of space in our quarantine tanks the fish were not quarantined on arrival, nor were they treated with any drugs.

The two cardinal clowns made their home in a large *Radianthus* anemone which originally had had pale pink tentacles with purple tips but which had faded to white with purple tips. It was of a different type from that which the clowns would inhabit in the wild. In addition to the other contents listed, there was a small lion fish added to the tank for a while but he died after we had also put in a large red starfish. (The starfish died and in dying gave off a mass of foam which frothed like detergent. This distressed the lion fish which jumped out of the tank in the night and was found in the morning dead on the floor.) We changed about half of the water in the tank after removing the foam and fitted a hood and a light. The tank, which was in a dark corner, had been receiving little direct light and absolutely no sunlight. The light which we fitted was a 24-inch TL.20W/33T. The partial water change referred to above took place early in November, i.e. about seven weeks before the actual spawning.

The two clowns started clearing the sand from their corner and showing interest in each other about four months after we had put them into the tank. We then discontinued putting the tank light on, for fear of disturbing them, but we continued to light the fish room on dull days and to keep the room lights on until late in the evening. The fish were by now in excellent condition, and a slight raggedness in the fins which we had noticed when we first received them had grown out. At no time had we given this pair any special attention, though they probably benefited from all the food which we had to shower into the tank to feed the very greedy *Cerianthus*. This consisted mainly of uncooked shrimp although it is possible that at some stage they received a little live brine shrimp. They had not, however, had this food immediately prior to spawning. We had also been feeding the tank with a proprietary liquid designed for young live-bearers. This was put into the water because we wanted to rear the *Astrophytons* and we had noticed that the clowns liked it and would gulp at it. They had also had occasional meals of live shrimps which we had put into the tank, both the common kind and a small 'glass'-like species which, however, they had difficulty in catching.

For some days before the actual spawning we had noticed that the clowns were very hungry and greedily seizing chopped shrimp from our fingers, even when we were trying to reach beyond them to feed the *Cerianthus* at the back of the tank. In fact, it became difficult to feed the latter because the clowns would arrest the food, whether held in our fingers or scattered, on the way over their heads.

We noticed that these fish had cleared a pit in the sand beneath the rock on which their anemone was lying and we then removed from this area a newly introduced (third) *Cerianthus* which was lying on the cleaned cement bottom of the tank immediately beneath their anemone. This space was about 3 to 4 inches long and 1½ to 2 inches wide and had been fanned out by the clowns during the preceding week. This was on Saturday, December 16, 1967 and the following account is taken from a diary kept at the time:

Sunday, 17.12.67. We went out at about 11.30 a.m. and remained away from home until 7.30 p.m. by which time it was dark. We then found that the clowns had spawned on the cement wall of the tank, at right angles to the cleaned sand area, and farther back, so that the anemone in which they rested was protecting the spawn with its tentacles. The fish were fanning the eggs with their fins, taking it in turns to do a run over them and then rubbing themselves on the underside of the anemone tentacles and repeating the process.

Once one of the fishes was seen rubbing its underneath on the tentacles so closely that it might have been cleaning itself. The anemone appeared to be thriving on all this attention and was puffing up and fluffing out its tentacles to touch the eggs. We wondered, in fact, whether this could have been in part the object of the clowns' performance – were they stimulating the anemone to encourage it to protect the spawn?

The eggs were bright-orange coloured, about half a millimetre in diameter but rather longer than round. A thin web of some transparent substance held them to the side of the tank but allowed them to move when fanned. At one stage both fish in turn seemed to be mouthing the eggs, or possibly breathing on them, but they did not harm them. The shape of the spawn mass was roughly circular, about 1½ inches in diameter, but the outline was ragged at the edges and not a true circle. We estimated that there were several hundred eggs but it was impossible to count them because they were partly hidden by the weaving of the anemone tentacles and also because the fish resented our interest. Different onlookers' estimates ranged from between 150 and 200 to about 500 eggs. When the spawn grew larger we could see better and then thought that the quantity would have been about 200.

Monday, 18.12.67. The anemone spread itself still further to protect the eggs and the clowns continued to fan them occasionally, and also to fan the anemone and take a roll in it, but their performance did not have so much urgency as previously and they did not seem to be working on the spawn to the same extent. When not fanning they remained in the anemone close to the eggs in a guard position. We saw one of the fish lay itself momentarily across the other at right angles in the anemone and also butt it with the under part of the body. Both fish swam amongst the tentacles in such a way as to encourage the anemone to cover the eggs and they did this whenever the tank was approached. They again ate greedily of chopped shrimp.

Tuesday, 19.12.67. The fish and spawn were photographed today and the fish did not seem to be unduly alarmed by ten flash photographs. In the evening we fed them with live shrimps but they would not venture far from their eggs and in the end we had to hold a shrimp by its tail for them to take. (We would not normally do this as we consider it cruel and most unfair to the shrimp, but we were anxious to get some live food into the clowns.) The fish which received the shrimp held it amongst the anemone tentacles to disable it and then chewed off the head. Possession of the shrimp passed from one clown to the other as first one and then the other wrested it away, but there was no quarrelling. The fish deliberately kept the shrimp away from the stomach of the anemone until they had finished with it. During this performance both turned occasionally to the eggs to breathe on them.

Friday, 22.12.67. The eggs have been getting noticeably darker and are now a reddish brown and longer.

Saturday, 23.12.67. We removed *Cerianthus,* corals, *Astrophyton* and most of the glass shrimps from the tank in order to safeguard the fry when hatched. In the evening, a friend from the University of Singapore came and took flash photographs of the spawn.

Monday, 25.12.67. The eyes of the eggs are now well-developed and the

116

eggs very elongate. They still wave in a protective web when fanned by the pectoral fins of the parent fish. Both parents appear to be attempting to force the anemone to move back and on repeated occasions have been seen to strain against it as though to push it away from the spawn. We have moved the rock with the anemone on it back very gently and gradually so that the eggs are completely free from the tentacles.

Tuesday, 26.12.67. Silver-white patches (possibly yolk sacs) are well formed on all eggs, in addition to eyes, and both parents are paying almost continuous attention to the spawn. They are repeating the forcing technique on the anemone and patrolling a narrow channel from which the sand has been fanned out between the wall of the tank and the anemone. The clowns make clicking noises as if annoyed. The anemone is more noticeably 'sticky' to the touch than we had remembered it to be.

Wednesday, 27.12.67. The eggs have obviously hatched during the night, but there is no sign of the fry. The parents appear to be guarding something but no fry can be seen. The anemone seems to have raised itself into a tent-like shape and on one side the 'roof' is supported by a piece of loose coral rock under the lip. There is a new cleared space visible under the rock at the back.

Thursday, 28.12.67. The situation is much the same as yesterday. Both the fish appear to be very plump, particularly the female, and it is suspected that a further spawning is not far away. The guarding procedure continues. Surely if the fry have survived they should emerge very shortly for food, as the yolk sacs must be exhausted by now? We have fed the tank with proprietary baby fish food. Late this evening we heard more clicking noises and both parents were pushing at the anemone with an apparent sense of urgency.

Saturday, 29.12.67. We think that we have solved the problem as to what happened to the fry. Discovered a large bottom fish which must have been in the tank for several months, right under the rock on which the clowns were living in their anemone. We suspect that this was the cause of their anger and the clicking noises – which they did not seem to make when we approached the tank. Perhaps this fish was also the clearer of the sand under the rock on 27th and the erector of the stone beneath the anemone 'tent'. These fish are cave dwellers, so that is possible. He has now been removed.

We hope that the clowns will spawn again despite the disruption of the tank during removal of the bottom fish.

The fish did not spawn again until January 22nd. We discovered the eggs at 7.15 p.m. which in Singapore is just after dark. The fish had previously been taking chopped shrimp very greedily and had been cleaning the wall of the tank. They had lately been kept rather in the dark because the male had an eye infection which we did not want to aggravate with too strong a light. Neither fish had had any live food fed to it for a month.

The development of the eggs and the behaviour of the fish followed the same pattern as previously until the ninth night when it became evident that the eggs were likely to hatch. We therefore decided to stay up to watch the hatching and the following is an account from our diary:

Midnight 31.1.68. There has been a small amount of cleaning action by the female, near the eggs. She has also been shivering and indulging in love play with the male. Both parents are mouthing the eggs and fanning them strongly as if trying to loosen the web and sometimes they brush it lightly with the ventral fins as they turn away from the egg mass at the completion of a 'sweep'.

2.15 a.m. 1.2.68. Fish are still mouthing the eggs and working on them with their fins, mother doing most of the work. The web has been loosened at one side. Both parents are hungry and eating waste food in the tank.

2.30 a.m. The female has several times mouthed the eggs and spat something which we could not see clear of the anemone and up to the surface of the water. She now brushes aside the male when he tries to fan. The anemone is very puffed and 'tented'.

2.35 a.m. Very small fry have appeared on the surface; we have taken some of these out and put them in a separate tank. Other small fry are seen to be swimming.

2.55 a.m. Both clowns are still working on the egg mass. Larger fry are now being hatched and there is no doubt that the mother spits them clear of the anemone to the top of the water where they soon become relatively strong and free swimming. If one sinks to the bottom the mother gives it another puff and sends it to the surface. One of the small fry which we have just now taken out of the tank measures about $2\frac{1}{2}$ millimetres and it is possible to see the orange colour of the clown fish through its silvery transparency.

5.40 a.m. All this time the mother has been continuing to spit the fry clear of the egg mass and beyond the anemone, but is now becoming tired and negligent and does not always succeed in spitting each one clear. Some have floated free of their own accord. We saw the male help himself to one from the egg mass and then to another and the female pushed him away before he could eat any more. We have taken some fry out of the tank with a net, and others we have siphoned off to put in separate tanks. The balance remains with the parents.

There was no sign of any fry in the morning. They could have perished for a number of reasons including lack of sufficient food of the correct type or the unsuitability of the seawater for such young fry due to the presence of bacteria harmful to very young fish. We hope some day to find the solution to this problem.

9. Tunicates and Sea Squirts

Tunicates and sea squirts have a tadpole-like larval stage during which they are free-swimming but they later lose their tails and settle down to a sedentary life. They qualify for inclusion in the phylum Chordata by reason of possessing a notochord whilst they are in this larval stage: later, they lose it. Their bodies are encased in either a gelatinous or leathery casing, the *tunica*.

Sea Squirts

The *tunica* of these creatures is often much wrinkled; they have a large pharynx which is perforated by gill slits and two siphons which are often retractable, one containing the inlet and the other the outlet. Sea squirts feed in much the same way as sponges by filtering the seawater which comes in through one siphon and goes out of the other. They often live together in groups and we find that they propagate themselves freely in our tanks. No special feeding is necessary.

Our local species are mostly drab-coloured outside and the leathery jacket can become covered with hairy mulm. When young these may be lovely soft colours with the light showing through. Even in the adult stage some species are attractive because of the pink-and-white striped lining to their throats. A type found in Macassar is purple and gold and most beautiful.

Sea squirts are often found in company with zoanthids or sponge and the first evidence of their presence in a clump of such animals may be when a jet of water squirts out from its centre. They will also grow on a variety of other materials such as shells, wood, seaweed, etc., and when sent to England they continue to do well there.

Other Tunicates

There are other types of tunicates which form encrusting colonies on rocks. They consist of gelatinous masses sharing a common tunic and are often brightly coloured. The general appearance of these compound tunicates is similar to that of a collection of small encrusting sponges. Like the sea squirts to which they are related, they spread freely in the tank and repropagate themselves when the original colonies die off. They are therefore very good value and, although they prefer some sunlight, seem able to thrive without it.

10. Reef-building (Madreporarian) Corals

No very deep understanding of coral biology is needed in order to keep a few corals in a tank but some knowledge of the subject may well increase the pleasure of watching these creatures. The following notes barely touch upon this field of study. Readers who wish to pursue it more scientifically are recommended to consult the works listed in the bibliography and more especially the scientific reports of the Great Barrier Reef Expedition, 1928–9.

The three main types of coral reef are:

Barrier reefs which are separated from the main shore by a lagoon,
Atolls which are circular or horseshoe-shaped reefs enclosing a lagoon,
Fringing reefs around coastlines or islands.

Most of our work has been done with specimens from the fringing reefs around Singapore and its islands. The best corals are found at depths where the sunlight can still penetrate: growth falls off as the water deepens. Reef colours are not particularly strong apart from those of the bright coral fishes and the purple undersides of anemones. Delicate pastel tints prevail, or reddish tones shading to brown, enlivened here and there by patches of vivid green.

Corals are members of the phylum Coelenterata and their origins go back many millions of years. Like other members of this group such as jellyfishes, anemones, sea fans and sea gooseberries, they possess nematocysts. These are minute poisoned harpoons attached by a thread to a capsule. The poison contained in corals is too weak to be felt by human beings, although one species of *Millepora* does inflict a mild sting. The nematocysts catch zooplankton upon which the corals feed.

Nearly all Madreporarian corals contain innumerable unicellular plants – symbiotic zooxanthellae – which carry out photosynthesis and are fed on excretory products from the corals. Zooxanthellae probably contribute more than any other factor to the success of corals in aquaria because they both help to remove the waste products from the corals and also produce oxygen. Light is essential to zooxanthellae, the incidence of which declines at depths where this is scarce. Corals will live without zooxanthellae but will not thrive, at least under aquarium conditions, when so deprived.

Corals are basically a thin layer of living animals on a large dead mineral skeleton. Individual members, or polyps, usually live together in colonies, organically connected to each other. (But some such as *Fungia* are non-colonial.) The body is virtually a sac enclosing the stomach surmounted by tentacles. There is no anus and undigested food is ejected from the mouth. Neither is there any respiratory nor blood system nor any specialized sensory organs; the nervous system is very primitive.

In some corals the tentacles (which contain the nematocysts) are the predominant feature. These corals will look very different after death. So also will those whose chief distinction is the length and beauty of the polyps, such as species of *Goniopora*. In this they differ from *Oulastrea crispata* of which the main features are the pattern formed by the corallites themselves and the dark skeleton. (The corallite or calyx forms the hard outer shell of the polyp; in some species corallites have common walls or they may merge into one another as in the 'brain' corals.) In the list at the end of this chapter we have described the corals by their predominant features when alive. The shape of the skeleton alone is rarely a good guide to the identity of a living coral.

A few corals such as *Millepora* belong to the class Hydrozoa, which is a primitive form, the body cavity being a simple enclosed sac having two types of polyps – feeding ones and smaller stinging ones. All remaining hard corals come under the classification Anthozoa, in which the body cavity is divided up into partitions (septa) and separated from the mouth by a pharynx. Most of the hard, reef-building corals and the sea anemones belong to the sub-class of Anthozoa known as Hexacorallia, whereas all the soft corals, including the gorgonians, belong to the sub-class Octocorallia (Alcyonaria).

Breeding

Most hard corals produce germ cells within the polyp and after fertilization the eggs hatch into minute free-swimming planulae. Many of these will be devoured by other sea creatures but some will survive to become new coral polyps. Reproduction can also be asexual by the budding off

123

of corals and we have frequently found new buds of *Fungia actiniformis* growing in our tanks.

So far as the actual mating process is concerned, Sheina Marshall records that:

*'In some species of colonial corals the sexes appear to be separate, whilst others are definitely hermaphrodite. In the hermaphrodite forms a single polyp may be male or female (at least at a given time), in which case it is the colony and not the individual which is hermaphrodite. . . .'

and also concludes that:

'The general rule amongst corals appears to be viviparity, the fertilized egg developing into a larva before extrusion from the parent polyp; but there are also cases in which ova and spermatozoa have been extruded as such.'

In our own tanks we have watched a phenomenon which seems to be connected with the breeding process of corals. They swell and then emit strings of slime which eventually disperse into the water. If one piece of coral starts to give off slime others will sometimes follow. It is not always easy, however, to judge whether this slime is all part of the breeding process or whether some of the corals are letting off mucus in order to trap planulae from others, as they will do when baby sea horses are discharged from the father's pouch. On one occasion we certainly watched the breeding process of one *Euphyllia fimbriata*.

Breeding started at about 10 p.m. one day in mid-April and finished two hours and a half later. First the tank became slightly cloudy and the coral concerned looked sick. This was a large one, about 12 × 8 inches with twenty-four colonies. Six of these were not much affected apart from having their tentacles more or less retracted. The tentacles of the other eighteen colonies became flabby and lifeless and shrank into the flesh surrounding the gastro-vascular cavities. This flesh cannot usually be seen because it is hidden by the tentacles which are long and waving. When breeding was about to start it became bloated and almost transparent, with the cavities widening so that it was possible to see into them. At intervals of about 5 to 10 minutes the eighteen colonies could be seen to heave in unison. Then the tentacles jerked upwards and clouds of

*Scientific reports of the Great Barrier Reef Expedition 1928–29.

white 'smoke' (spermatozoa – or planulae[?]) then issued from the cavities, spreading towards the surface for about 6 to 8 inches before it dispersed. The six half-retracted colonies made a rather feeble attempt to join in this emission.

Some time later a *Goniopora* six inches away began to look slightly swollen and its polyps drooped. Corals farther from that which was breeding presently started to react, including two smaller groups of *Euphyllia fimbriata* which behaved in the same way as the large one except that emission was less prolific and not sustained for so long. A group of *Hydnophora rigida* extended its polyps and a cuplike *Turbinaria* started to send out strings of slime. The fishes took very little notice.

A friend in England to whom we had sent a piece of *Turbinaria crater* from Singapore reported that he watched two of the polyps apparently mating in his tank. They bent over so that their heads embraced and then remained locked together in this fashion for about two hours. As they disengaged he noted through his spy-glass that the central cavity of each polyp had been erected to come into contact with that of the other.

Recovery and Rate of Growth

Corals do not all grow at the same rate, nor does a coral have a constant rate of growth: they have rest periods. Young ones normally grow more quickly than older and corals which are in natural surroundings will make more progress than those kept unnaturally. A head of *Lobophyllia hemprichii* which we had increased its size by one-third in 4 to 5 months. We also kept a piece of the delicate *Pectinia lactuca* which had been badly crushed. In less than six weeks this very brittle coral had completely recovered and new growth had hidden the bruised parts. There have been other cases where coral which had lost its zooxanthellae and become colourless has recovered after six weeks in more natural conditions with a reasonable amount of sunlight. Corals will also fold and change shape whilst in a tank, presumably to enable them to adapt to the local conditions and to take advantage of whatever light there is.

Selection and Care of Corals

We have listed and described some of the common hard corals found in Indo-Pacific waters and which are likely to appeal to aquarists; also included are coloured photographs in the 'live' state of some of those which have survived in our tanks. Black-and-white photographs are provided showing dead coral skeletons.

The hardiest corals for tank use are: *Alveopora, Fungia, Goniopora, Oulastrea, Trachyphyllia, Tubastrea* and *Turbinaria.*

All the above, except *Trachyphyllia,* are reasonably resistant to damage by fish. Most people will want to include at least one 'brain coral'. 'Brain coral' is a loose, unscientific name for those of the meandrine corals whose ridges form patterns which look like brains. *Platygyra lamellina* is the easiest to keep and small specimens can sometimes be found. It has green valleys with brown ridges as a general rule, although it may be greenish-brown all over. We have indicated in our list which are the other 'brain corals'. *P. lamellina* is particularly liable to fade on any side which does not get sufficient light and it should be placed so as not to be overshadowed by other coral.

Some corals extend their polyps mostly in the dark. These still need light during the daytime. Both in the wild and in our tanks we have noticed, however, that these supposedly night-blooming corals will open during daylight hours if there is an influx of new plankton for them to devour. On the reef this may happen when there is a strong current flowing, especially at or near monsoon times when zooplankton is at its most prolific. Most of the corals whose main beauty is in their extended polyps are day-blooming types,* so that in making your choice of corals for the tank it is not necessary to consider at what time they open.

In our experience, only the following corals are completely safe to put on sand: *Fungia* (all species), *Herpolitha limax, Oulastrea crispata, Polyphyllia talpina* and *Trachyphyllia geoffroyi.*

All others must be placed on a hard rock foundation or direct on to the tank bottom. If there are large fish in the tank ensure that they cannot dislodge any corals which have been put upon rock, lest these fall to the sand. Watch also that the sand does not become stirred up so as to submerge the corals. Wrasses are particularly guilty of causing this kind of nuisance. They dive under the sand to sleep and this causes it to swirl and eddy around the tank.

Smaller fishes may need branching types of coral in which to roost at night and through which they can escape when chased by their larger enemies. The problem here is that some fish will eat *Pocillopora damicornis* which is the hardiest of the arborescent corals. When we had this coral in our tanks we used to call it the 'bread-and-butter' coral because it seemed to be the staple diet of the Chaetodontidae (except for *Chelmon rostratus*). If such coral dies because it has been eaten it is not necessary

---

*An exception to this rule is *Tubastrea aurea* and its relative *T. diaphana,* but both of these corals are attractive, though less so when not blooming.

to remove it from the tank because the skeleton is unlikely to decompose and cause contamination; if left it will soon become covered with algae and look very attractive. *P. damicornis* often has attractive orange-red crabs living in its branches and these provide a useful scavenging service which keeps the coral free from decaying matter. As a general principle, commensal animals such as these should be allowed to remain unless you know that they are harmful.

Some corals will serve the various species of *Amphiprion* as substitutes for anemones if the latter are in short supply. These clown fishes will play in the long tentacles of *Fungia actiniformis* or will sometimes use *Goniopora* instead. We have seen a very small *A. bicinctus* biting and pulling at the tentacles of a *Euphyllia* without apparently doing it any harm and he was enjoying himself.

It is essential to keep any anemone or *Cerianthus* as far away from your corals as possible; both have tentacles which will kill the living polyps and furthermore if either creature should chance to settle upon a coral it will suffocate its host. Similarly, corals can be killed by the nematocysts of neighbouring corals.

Corals should not be kept out of water for longer than is absolutely necessary and whilst out of the tank (or in it, for that matter) should not be subjected to sudden changes of temperature. They should be handled as little and as gently as possible. If it is necessary to lift a coral it should be grasped by the hard base; the fingers should avoid contact with the fleshy part. Coral should preferably not be put down on any surface outside the tank, but if a table has to be used this must be clean, free from contamination with detergents, dyes and insecticides and made of a substance not subject to corrosion by seawater. Coral will not tolerate insecticides nor other chemicals and for this reason we never allow our tank room to be sprayed against mosquitoes.

If the fish in a tank need treatment with substances such as methylene blue, copper sulphate or other drugs, they must be removed and treated separately.

Whilst a coral is out of water it should not be subjected to strong sunlight nor should it be put down where insects such as ants may attack it.

When frightened or shocked coral gives off slime which must be removed from the tank or collecting bucket without further disturbing the coral.

New specimens need to be quarantined for at least fourteen days since they were last in contact with fish. Coral itself cannot, so far as we know, contract any fish diseases, but it may well play host to them. The quarantine period recommended is to protect the fish.

Coral should only be obtained from an experienced and trusted collector or through an established aquarist specializing in marine work.

It is no good expecting that your corals will look their best at all times. They can be very unpredictable and a specimen which will thrive in one tank will go off colour in another, even when placed in an apparently similar position. Or it may decide to rest for a while. Some will die off on the side not exposed to light and most will do so where they touch each other. One coral should never be placed so that it touches or stands upon another. A fairly high density of coral can be accepted in a tank but it is not necessary to have a very great number or variety of specimens to make a tank look attractive.

11. Some Common Hard Corals of the Indo-Pacific

Alveopora excelsa. This is a delicate-looking coral and most attractive, rather like a small hump of daisies. The polyps are more fragile looking than those of *Goniopora* and have shorter stems. They are grey or similarly subdued colours, with white tips. It blooms profusely during the daytime. Colonies are rarely more than about 2 to 3 inches in diameter. It is hardy and very satisfactory in the tank, but difficult to find on the reef.

Euphyllia fimbriata. Full-grown specimens have long, continuous wandering valleys surmounted by luxuriant tentacles, and are normally brown or greyish-brown – occasionally greenish – with light tips to the tentacles. It is more difficult to establish in the tank than *E. glabrescens* but once settled does well.

Euphyllia glabrescens. Before we knew the scientific name for this coral we called it 'tassel coral' because of the long tentacles which look like beaded tassels. These are normally brown or greyish-brown – more rarely green – with pale-coloured tips.

There are several other species of *Euphyllia* found locally which we have not yet identified.

Favia speciosa. This is a humped coral, usually pale-green with corallites evenly distributed all over the hump. The hearts of the corallites are bright green.

Favites abdita. Frequently this has a humped shape; its corallite walls are more angular in outline than those of *Favia*, with the corallites closely clustered all over the surface. Usually pale yellowish-green with deeper colour at the heart of each corallite.

Fungia

All the species of this coral make good tank decoration, both when blooming and when dormant. They can be placed on sand and are low, which makes them particularly suitable for the front of the tank.

Fungia actiniformis. This round cartwheel-type sand coral is usually about 1 to 3 inches in diameter, but can grow much larger. The most common colour is brown with fleshy pale-brownish body having very long, thick tentacles tipped with creamy colour. Green ones are sometimes found.

Fungia echinata. This is similar to the foregoing except that it is boat-shaped with shorter, almost transparent tentacles, and a brown or greyish body.

Fungia fungites. The thin tentacles of this coral appear to be more extended at night and are almost transparent, with narrow tips. Sometimes it has a very pretty crimson rim. Its body is pale-brown or biscuit-coloured, normally round, but sometimes adopting pretty flower-like outlines. We usually place it on a rock base, because though it will tolerate sand it is most often found upon rocks.

Fungia repanda. This is almost indistinguishable from the previous coral, except that on the underneath the radial ridges join together to form more conspicuous and less sharp edges. There must, we think, be corals of this type with crimson edges similar to *F. fungites,* but we have not yet found any.

Goniastrea

There are three species commonly found on local reefs but we have not been successful in keeping any for very long.

Goniastrea pectinata. This usually forms a green hump similar to *Favia* but with smaller corallites having common walls. There is a tendency for some of them to extend lengthwise and to wander.

Goniastrea benhami. This is similar but has a higher proportion of such extended corallites and the 'valleys' are longer.

130

Goniastrea retiformis. Similar to *G. pectinata*, but this has smaller coral-lites with thinner walls between them.

Goniopora

The differences between the species are slight, biologically speaking, although the habit of growth varies. All members of this genus have very long, daisy-like polyps ranging in colour from pale-green or pale-gold to beige or lavender or, but rarely, brownish-red. These corals are very hardy and satisfactory in the tank. They normally blossom in daylight and when the tank lights are on, but we have had one or two which would only open at night. Some species are liable to be very irregular in shape with thickish, stumpy projections and short branches; others can look like a dog's bone. The most common and easily recognized is:

Goniopora lobata. This is usually hump-shaped with long-stemmed polyps 3/6 of a millimetre in diameter.

Heliopora coerulea. A fairly hardy coral usually found in closely clustered groups of branches about 1 inch thick with blunted roundish tops. The polyps are virtually invisible except to give an overall brown appearance to the coral which has a greyish-blue skeleton showing through where any branches are broken. The skeleton remains blue after death, unlike all the other corals in this list, which have white skeletons. The coral is also unlike the others in that it is a member of the sub-class of Anthozoa called Octocorallia, whereas they belong to the sub-class Hexacorallia. *H. coerulea* is usually host to aquarium scavengers, crabs, etc., and the smaller fishes will play through its branches.

Herpolitha limax. A hardy coral, this is more or less boat-shaped and roughly resembles *Fungia echinata*; but whereas the latter has one central mouth this coral has a number of mouths hidden between the ridges, which are shorter than those of *F. echinata* and vary in length. Usually it is of a brownish or greyish colour but may sometimes be green. It is a useful coral for standing on the sand in front of the tank and adds interest to a collection of sand corals.

Hydnophora exesa. This is a most attractive coral, not hardy, which we have recently succeeded in keeping in our tanks. It grows in rather thin 'plates' of irregular shape, sometimes forming small peaks. Small, thin,

131

tooth-like projections stick up all over the surface and small fuzzy polyps obscure these projections. The colours are chocolate-brown, a misty blue-grey or pale-bluish jade-green. There is also a mossy-coloured one.

Hydnophora rigida. Similar to the above, but with a branching form, this also we have recently domesticated. It is attractive when established, but a difficult coral which needs careful watching lest it die and contaminate the tank.

Lobophyllia hemprichii. A large, beautiful 'brain' coral with wide, rather deep valleys, this normally has brown ridges above mossy-green valleys, but may also be paler green. In life it is difficult to tell the difference between this and *Symphyllia nobilis,* unless there is dead coral beneath the living head which enables the sharp-toothed septa to be measured. In *L. hemprichii* these project about twice as far above the ridge as those of *S. nobilis* and the walls of the valley are thicker. Success with this coral probably depends upon finding a small enough piece which will grow up in the tank – it is a fast grower when conditions are right. We would not describe it as hardy.

Merulina ampliata. A thin, often saucer-shaped coral, with small projections breaking the surface which is ridged in small valleys, this is normally brown or a glorious vivid bluish-green. The coral dies slowly and has to be removed to avoid poisoning the tank. We are persevering with it, but in the meanwhile we cannot recommend it.

Mycedium tubifex. A small, thin, plate-like coral which forms irregular scrolls around rocks or branches of dead coral, it is browny-grey with difficult-to-distinguish polyps, and very delicate.

Oulastrea crispata. A dainty small coral which encrusts rocks, this is usually found in muddy sand. The corallites are a greyish colour and project very little. A dark skeleton shows between them giving an effect as of a rock decorated with a design of closely packed small daisy heads in low relief. The coral looks much the same alive or dead except that in life it has small colourless tentacles but these are difficult to see. It is hardy and a good front-of-the-tank piece.

Pavona crassa. An exciting specimen which grows to great size on the reef, this has large plates or leaves combining to form a cabbage-like outline with smaller subsidiary leaves growing out of the larger ones and forming niches which in the wild often harbour tube worms. We have only succeeded with the smaller specimens but once acclimatized these are very impressive. The colour is usually brown but sometimes brownish-green, the small, nearly colourless polyps giving a downy bloom to the coral. Fish and crabs often live between the leaves and in the wild it is sometimes the home of moray eels. This coral is not hardy, but when it starts to die off it will not poison the tank. It is also possible to discern when it is happening, by the white patches, which slowly spread on the brown. Algae will grow over these white patches so that even when dead it is an attractive and useful specimen, because the fish like to play in it and it remains a good place in which to group tube worms.

Pavona frondifera. This is similar to the foregoing, but much smaller. We have not yet managed to keep a specimen.

Pectinia lactuca. A most beautiful coral, its bare skeleton is so thin as to be transparent. It has fluted 'petals' which join together to form flowerlike shapes and when dead the effect is often reminiscent of a white peony. In life a fleshy blue-green tissue covers the coral. The individual polyps have mouths in the centre of the flower shape and are not discernible, as a general rule. When extended they are colourless.

Platygyra lamellina. A 'brain' coral normally hump-shaped or the shape of a head, it has a maze of short, narrow valleys enclosed at each end. Not to be confused with the larger, deeper valleyed corals such as *Lobophyllia* or *Symphyllia*. The valley walls are brown and the valleys green; sometimes it may be greenish-brown all over. This is the easiest of the 'brain' corals to keep and small specimens are sometimes found. The attraction of this coral is in the pattern formed by the valley walls. Though easier to keep than others of the same type it is not hardy.

Pocillopora damicornis. This coral is bush-shaped with closely packed branches. In life the white skeleton is covered with darkish-brown polyps giving it a rather fuzzy appearance; when dead the strong but delicately formed branches are still attractive.

It is the most popular of all the corals as a food for the Chaetodontidae. most of whom will strip it bare in a very short time. When killed in this way it will not contaminate the tank.

133

Podabacia crustacea. This is a thin, plate-like coral which folds itself into saucer or chalice formations. The polyps are difficult to distinguish but give a bluish-grey bloom to the biscuit-coloured body. We kept one which was 9 inches deep and the small fishes liked to play in it. It is not hardy but it is very attractive.

Polyphyllia talpina. A hardy coral, this is usually boat-shaped, rather like *Herpolitha limax* but with smaller and less distinct ridges. Its tentacles are brownish, greyish or greenish, short and delicate with small cream-coloured tips. This coral seems to lend itself to distortion of the shape and we have had one with three fingers and another arched to look like a hen with a small head. It is uninteresting, but hardy and useful as a contrast to the more robust sand corals.

Porites lutea. A semi-hardy, hump-like coral, this is usually pale yellowish-green, brownish-green or pinkish-fawn, the polyps small and almost invisible. It is not interesting in itself but sometimes harbours delicate small tube worms.

Porites nigrescens. Otherwise known as the 'staghorn' coral, this is usually fawn in colour and not very attractive except for the small tube worms which it often shelters and also for the rather distinctive shape of the branches. We have succeeded with only very small young specimens. Larger pieces have all died and when this happens there is a tendency for contamination to spread rapidly through the tank. It does not look a very live coral at any time and deterioration is therefore liable to go undetected.

Psammocora contigua. A very attractive small chocolate-brown coral sometimes with an almost apple-green bloom, it has fairly thick leaves which are prettily fluted and the shape is similar to *Pavona frondifera*. Tube worms and small marine creatures will live in it. It is hardier than *P. frondifera* but not easy to keep.

Symphyllia nobilis. This is a 'brain' coral similar to *Lobophyllia hemprichii* but with less thick valley walls. The head is more compactly rounded. *S. nobilis* is usually green with brown ridges or pale greyish-green with the colour darkening in the valleys. It is difficult to find a small piece and when very small it does not look like a 'brain' coral; in this, also, it resembles *L. hemprichii*. It is not hardy.

134

Trachyphyllia geoffroyi. This coral has the most varied colour range of all our local corals and is one of the easiest – possibly *the* easiest – to keep. It is irregular in outline with thick, undulating edges. Often a colony will form itself into a hump. Small individual specimens are sometimes more flower-shaped. The tentacles mostly show at night but the beauty is in the iridescent effect of the fleshy body, especially when the coral swells. It then becomes almost transparent and shows up the varied colours. These can be a bright, fairly deep green, lime-green, creamy-grey, green with a pink stripe running around the edge, peachy colour shot with pink, a pale golden-brown with cream or deep brown-ish-crimson. It is satisfactory on sand but very liable to attack by most of the Chaetodontidae.

Tubastrea

We know only two species of *Tubastrea* and there is a difficulty in that some corals which are locally classified as *Tubastrea* are considered elsewhere to belong to the *Dendrophyllia* genus.

Tubastrea aurea. These are small delicate corals in groups or clusters, whose colour varies from primrose through orangy-pink to flaming-orange. If the polyps are dormant the corallites look like colourful little roundish buttons, often less than 10 millimetres in diameter. When extended the tentacles form petals of bright golden-yellow but they do not normally come out except at night or when there is abundant plankton or other suitable food in the water. This coral is usually found beneath rocks and may prefer to be in the shade for a good deal of the time, though we have seen it blooming in sunshine on the reef. It is hardy but difficult to find, and it is subject to long rest periods between blooming and particularly dislikes standing on sand. But it is too small to cause trouble in the tank if it dies and thoroughly recommended. A small papillated nudibranch the same colour as the *Tubastrea* preys upon it. We have known this coral to reproduce in the tank but have not seen the breeding process.

Tubastrea diaphana. Similar to the foregoing but black or dark-brown, this coral has a sheen which makes it look almost bronze in some lights. It blooms at night, and also hates sand.

Turbinaria

T. mollis and *T. peltata* are thoroughly satisfactory, hardy corals. Unless they are resting or sick they mostly bloom all day (or in some few cases all night – we have not managed to fathom why occasionally we get a night blooming specimen). Their only fault is that they sometimes take long rests between periods of blooming. The main body of the coral can be pale pinkish-brown, greenish-brown, pale-yellow, deeper-yellow or almost grey. *T. crater* is more delicate than either of these two species.

Turbinaria crater. This is mainly found in cup-like or chalice form and is most frequently brownish, with evenly spaced corallites dotted liberally over its body which are smaller than those of the other two species.

Turbinaria mollis. Normally folded into a cup-like shape with more conspicuous projecting corallites over the whole surface of the coral, its polyps are usually yellow, giving a soft, furry appearance. When first we collected this beautiful coral we nicknamed it the 'mimosa' coral.

Turbinaria peltata. This is similar to *T. mollis* but with more irregularly shaped edges and larger corallites clustered densely around the edges and less generously distributed over the centre of the coral. Its polyps are also usually yellow.

12. Cerianthus, Anemones and Zoanthids

All these creatures belong to the same biological class as corals – Anthozoa. Their anatomy is roughly similar to that of a coral polyp.

Cerianthus

Most species of *Cerianthus* have long tentacles and all of them live in membraneous tubes buried in the sand, usually just below the level of the lowest spring tides. The best specimens are found in clean water where there are strong currents. Their colour is usually pale: white, gold, paler-yellow, occasionally pale-green or brownish. Some have different-coloured centres. These creatures are unsuitable for community tanks unless carefully screened, because they can kill coral polyps with a touch and will lash out to capture and devour small fishes. We have not yet discovered any small fish which is safe from them. Sometimes the tentacles may droop; at others they will wave around gracefully or curl themselves up at the ends into tight ringlets. Whatever the species of *Cerianthus* we have in our tanks they are always popular with visitors who describe them as exotic, savage, flower-like or just plain evil but everyone agrees that they are beautiful. There is no doubt about their hardiness and when a new tube is needed they will fashion one from the sand of the tank. The old tube then rots away without causing contamination. An occasional change of sand and water should be provided and a good supply of coral rock to compensate for the lack of living coral (otherwise the tank will not balance).

Anemones

Sand Anemones. There are some anemones which look very much like species of *Cerianthus* and bury themselves in the sand in the same way, but without benefit of tubes. These are mostly dull-coloured creatures with short tentacles. As this type is of no interest to the clown fishes they are a waste of space in the tank.

137

The most satisfactory of the sand anemones are those belonging to the genus *Radianthus*. These spread themselves over the sand with the pedal disc anchored on a convenient piece of rock just below the surface. Some are very deep-pink with carmine tips, others greyish-white, similarly tipped, or paler-pink – these may have a mauvish tinge. The tentacles are more pointed than those of the larger types of rock anemones, which tend to have rounded and even swollen tips. *Radianthus* are useful in a tank because they will settle on rock or sand and are acceptable to the clown fishes. Some of the paler ones seem inclined to lose colour in captivity and become white. This does not affect their usefulness: the anemone used by our breeding cardinal clowns was a *Radianthus* which had faded.

Rock Anemones. The larger specimens can be very difficult to extricate from the crevices in the rock into which they have inserted their pedal discs and they may completely disappear when approached. There is a glorious rust-red one or a more common type with green tentacles and white 'beads' at the tips. Others are a greyish-green. Many have beautiful reddish-purple undersides.

An attractive smaller anemone is also found on the rocks; this has thin green up-curved tentacles and a brown centre.

Stoichactis. This anemone seems equally at home on rocks or sand. It is the largest of those which we have found and specimens of 3 to 4 feet in diameter are not uncommon. The clown fishes, when in the wild at least, seem to prefer it to any other. Apart from an occasional electric blue or navy blue one the colours are drab. The densely packed short tentacles have a powerful sting. Small specimens are hard to find and we have noticed that fish (including various *Amphiprion* species) kept in captivity with the large ones rarely flourish.

Boloceroides (Swimming Anemones). We have only had two of these, each about 9 centimetres in diameter. They were greyish-green and we found them near an inshore reef in muddy water. When these creatures swim they rise vertically then propel themselves by the action of the tentacles. They can also move by rolling along the sand. Because of their exceptional mobility they are not recommended for a community tank.

Reproduction of Anemones. In some species the young grow up inside the parent until it 'explodes' young anemones into the tank. If you see a

138

stream of mucus issuing from an anemone or a milky-looking fluid coming from the central cavity – do not interfere with it. This will in all likelihood be spermatozoa which, if not gobbled up by the fishes, may in time produce new anemones. We frequently find new young ones in our tank without having seen this process, however. Asexual reproduction takes place by budding and separation from the foot disc or less frequently by splitting.

The Relationship between Clown Fish and Anemones. Much has been written about the relationship between clown fish and their anemones and there is no doubt that this is beneficial to both parties. In return for using the anemone as a refuge, a larder and a bed – and also to protect their spawn – the clowns provide it with food and stimulation. They will revive it when sick by biting or fanning the tentacles. In this latter respect the fire clowns are far more assiduous than some other species. All will desert a sick anemone when it starts to die.

The anemone is incapable of any 'feelings' with regard to the fish to which it plays host. It has no eyes, brain nor circulatory system and only a limited nervous or reflex system triggered by contact. The reaction to any stimulus is purely mechanical – a contraction of the powerful muscles when attacked or disturbed and action of the nematocysts to sting anything which brushes the tentacles.

Fish have a brain and are a very much higher form of life, but their association with anemones is purely one of expediency. They may possibly regret the loss of an anemone – if, indeed, they are capable of regret – but it would at most be for the loss of a chattel. A clown will not hesitate to move to another more attractive anemone. Indeed, there is frequent rivalry for a new one, especially if it has more sting or is larger than the others. Experience suggests that anemones lose some of their stinging power after a while in captivity. The 'boss' clowns will fight off all other contenders and attempt to deny the smaller fish the right to roll in the anemones during daytime, but at night they permit them to sleep within the safety of the tentacles. Or perhaps the young ones sneak in when their elders are too sleepy to assert their rights.

If an anemone is moved or moves around the tank the clowns do not necessarily move with it, although they tend to do so. We had one family of common clowns who remained curtseying up and down for weeks near the spot which their anemone had vacated despite the presence of other unoccupied ones in the vicinity. In that case we had moved the anemone and it is possible that the fish had lost it, but they

139

will sometimes behave in a similar way when dispossessed by a larger neighbour.

We have seen no evidence to support the theory that clowns feed their anemones before they themselves eat and we doubt in any event whether the feeding process is deliberate. They will certainly seize the first piece of food which comes their way at feeding time, hide it in the outer tentacles of an anemone and dash back for more. Our view, however, is that this a procedure similar to that adopted by squirrels with nuts. Clowns will, if they remember, return to their anemones to retrieve the food even when it is just about to disappear into the central cavity. This makes sense in relation to reef conditions. Food supplies are irregular and liable to be swept away quickly in the strong currents. During times of temporary abundance, therefore, the fish must grab all that it can and where better to hide pieces too large for immediate consumption?

We have also known clowns to drive their prey into an anemone. In the case of live shrimps they will bite off the legs or eyes and then hold their victim amongst the tentacles until it is dead or otherwise rendered incapable of further resistance. They thereupon tear away at the flesh and break it down to more manageable proportions. The anemone may benefit from any residue, but only when the clowns are completely satisfied.

We do not believe that clowns actually lure fish into anemones. Those big enough to prey upon them are likely to be too large to be caught and held by the tentacles. Even the far more formidable *Cerianthus* does not appear to harm fish of more than about 5 inches in size.

Clowns – in the wild at least – are certainly selective in the type of anemone which they inhabit. *A. percula* for example appear to favour *Stoichactis*, which are large anemones with many shortish rather thin tentacles and a vicious sting. Those found locally are usually a dull-fawn colour. This is the only species in which we have found fry measuring half an inch or less in length. Larger *A. percula* can be found in other types of anemone but we suspect that they prefer *Stoichactis* for breeding. We have also on one occasion found fully mature specimens of *A. sebae* in much shallower water than usual, in company with a giant specimen of this anemone, nearly 3 feet in diameter. It could be that these clowns also use it for breeding. *A. ephippium* and others of the larger species favour anemones growing deep in the rocks, including the type with 'beaded' tentacles, both for living and for breeding.

The colourful *Radianthus* anemones which grow in the sand or on top of rocks do not seem to be favoured by any clowns in the wild, but are accepted gladly in captivity. We had a pair of cardinal clowns breeding in one and they were using the tentacles in the care of the spawn.

In our experience, spawn is laid within reach of the tentacles of the home anemone. We have suspected, from watching the action of the parents, that they may have been trying to impregnate the eggs with mucus from the anemone. During hatching the mother fish spits or blows the newly hatched fry clear of the anemone, but as she tires some youngsters will fall into it and we have seen them slip down between the tentacles without suffering any apparent harm.

We do not think that, as a general rule, *Amphiprion* fry inhabit the same anemones as their parents. It is only rarely that we have found very small specimens in the same anemone as adults and in such cases the anemone has always been very large. When we have tried to keep small specimens (say about half an inch long) in a tank with full-grown ones, they have never thrived. On the other hand, if we keep these babies in a tank of their own, well furnished with anemones, they flourish and grow rapidly.

What is it that protects clowns from the nematocysts of anemones? There is reason to believe that this immunity may be acquired at a very early age – possibly in the spawn stage – if it is not inherited. Some experts think that clowns possess a special mucus which makes them immune or else immobilizes the nematocysts.

A nematocyst can be discharged only once and used ones are discarded and replaced by new ones. As clowns spend most of their time snuggling and wriggling amongst their anemone tentacles it seems unlikely that the nematocysts are discharged each time they are touched. Surely no anemone could replace nematocysts at that rate? If this argument is sound, then it would suggest that the clowns have some means of immobilizing the nematocysts. Local species of *Amphiprion* are said to be vulnerable to certain anemones found in foreign waters such as the *Plumose* anemone. They are certainly not immune to long tentacled hydroids or to *Cerianthus*.

There is no doubt that clowns well settled in a favourite anemone gain a sensual delight from contact with the tentacles and it is a pleasure to watch them snuggle deeply into them at night. If the tentacles are too short they will lie on top of them instead, as on a feather bed. Presumably it is the fishes' gill action and the fact that in sleep they move continuously, although almost imperceptibly, which prevents them from being swallowed. Or they may be capable of escaping from the gullet. When collecting *Stoichactis* we have known small clowns to emerge into our buckets from the very centre of these anemones in circumstances which have suggested that they could only have been taking refuge in the gullet itself.

Although the clowns seem to gain the major advantage from their relationship with anemones the latter undoubtedly do benefit from scraps of unclaimed food. In addition, the constant action of the fish probably assists aeration and the diffusion of waste products: having no circulatory system the anemone can only rely on the diffusion of oxygen from surrounding water and the pummelling of the clowns must assist this. Certainly anemones thrive best in tanks with attendant clowns, probably for this reason.

The various species of *Amphiprion* are not the only fish to dwell within anemone tentacles. At least one other member of the Pomacentridae family does so – that is *Dascyllus trimaculatus*. We have caught these small fish hovering in what appeared to be dangerous proximity to anemones in the wild. Later, in our tanks at night, we have seen them snuggled up against the underneath sides of the anemones. Young specimens of less than half an inch in length have also been caught within the tentacles of *Stoichactis*. Dr Fishelson tells us that in the Red Sea *D. trimaculatus* breeds on stones and in shallow caves but that the young fry invade sea anemones when they reach a size of about half an inch. In our experience these fish do not use anemones to anything like the same extent as the various *Amphiprion* species do, and it may be that the association is mainly in the juvenile stages or when the fish needs a refuge in emergency.

We have also seen a small member of one of the *Gobiodon* species – little fish which make their home amongst the branches of *Acropora* and similar corals – resting on a small pink anemone in one of our tanks. Later we saw a small glass prawn straying over the same territory. This anemone had been without any clowns for some time, however, which may have accounted for its tolerating these intruders.

Feeding of Anemones and Cerianthus. Feeding is dealt with elsewhere, but we will repeat the warning: Food should never be dropped directly into the centre of an anemone or *Cerianthus* but should be allowed to fall into the water within reach of the tentacles. Both creatures have a complicated feeding system which will be upset if they are fed by stuffing food into the gastro-vascular cavity.

Sea Mushrooms. These are a type of small anemone, usually about 1 to 2 inches in diameter and often mushroom-shaped. They are found encrusting rocks, often rather unsafe, porous ones. The colour may be a bright bluish-green, paler and more yellowish, brown or sometimes brown with blue or peacock streaks. Sea mushrooms often appear to be luminescent at night. The normal process of propagation appears to be by budding and division. In this case the foot part shrinks to a thin line of slime and the 'parent' shrivels. When it again expands there will be a new individual where the foot has split. During this process the animal looks very unhealthy and smells unpleasant. We think that it is likely that sea mushrooms can also reproduce sexually. They spread readily in a tank.

Zoanthids

These are often referred to as encrusting anemones but have no pedal disc and are usually colonial. When contracted the polyps look an unattractive dirty greyish colour. They open out into little daisy-like shapes and the colours vary from brown to pale-green, pale-pink, slate-grey, darker-green or olive-green. They sometimes have different coloured centres. The size is usually less than half an inch in diameter and 1 inch in height. Zoanthids are very satisfactory in tanks with plenty of light but care must be taken with the rock upon which they are found. This is often porous and spongy and liable to harbour corruption. Sponges found on the rock should be removed but not sea squirts which are also often found with zoanthids and help to promote tank health. Sometimes zoanthids can be peeled from the rock without damaging them.

13. Crustaceans

The sub-phylum Crustacea contains about 2,500 species but we are only concerned with a very few, our interest being limited to crabs, prawns and shrimps.

Crabs

We like crabs, even the larger ones, and we admire their fighting spirit when we meet them on the reef flats; but we only collect the smallest species. These creatures will grow very rapidly in a tank, but as their size increases so do their appetites and they will damage coral and plants.

The smaller ones can be very attractive. Sponge crabs are delightful miniature specimens with a passion for camouflage. They will cover the top of the carapace with living zoanthids or sponge. If these materials are not available we have known the crab to use a discarded piece of tube worm casing worn crosswise like a Napoleon-type hat. We once lost such a little crab, which had decked itself with nodding zoanthids, and when much later we found it the zoanthids had been jettisoned in favour of a close-fitting cap of blue sponge. However hard we try to grow sponge it is always difficult and unreliable, whereas these little creatures can not only keep it alive, but tailor it as they will.

Some of the smaller spider crabs found in seaweed remain small and harmless. They often encourage green algae to grow on their backs. These are quite attractive but there are larger spider crabs which grow into monsters – even attacking sleeping fishes. One such creature grew to nearly 6 inches. He had decked himself with blobs of blue and red sponge and we saw him tear to pieces an *Amphiprion percula* – which had been sick, certainly, but which we were not sure was dead before he started to devour it. We had had some *Tubastrea aurea* damaged in the same tank and suspected that he might be the culprit, so we gave him to two scientists who were studying that coral. He then confounded us by biting off a piece of their *Tubastrea* and hastily spitting it out again.

144

23. Blue-green wrasse swimming over unidentified coral (possibly a species of *Symphyllia*). We do not recommend this wrasse as suitable for a tank.

24. Golden wrasse over small but fully extended *Goniopora* – note the smaller polyps and more subdued colouring of the little greenish *Alveopora excelsa* slightly to the left. The coral immediately above the small pink anemone is a small piece of *Lobophyllia hemprichii*. A small piece of *Pavona crassa* is to the rear and right of the *Goniopora*. *Photograph by the author*

25. *Pectinia lactuca*
   Photograph by the author

26. Example of budding off of young *Fungia* from skeleton of parent – at a
   later stage these little corals will detach themselves and fall clear
   Photograph by the author

Swimming crabs are rather clumsy but young plump specimens are attractive. The common local species is *Neptunus pelagicus*, which has a habit of burying itself with just the eyes twinkling above the sand. It has a hearty appetite and will rapidly launch itself to the surface at feeding time, floundering upwards with the paddle-like claws thrashing.

The small red crabs which live in the arborescent corals such as *Pocillopora* are also attractive and harmless and we have known them to outlive their host coral when this has been eaten by fishes.

The family Paguridae or hermit crabs make their homes in the empty shells of univalves. Small specimens are attractive but if you wish to keep them you will need a supply of suitable empty shells for them to inhabit when they get larger. We do not think that it is practicable to keep them unless you can return them to the sea or give them to a public aquarium when they get too large.

Prawns and Shrimps

The most attractive of these for aquarium use are the banded coral shrimps (*Stenopus hisbidis*) which live within the tentacles of anemones. We have not found these locally but have had several pairs of another species commonly called 'anemone prawns'. They have white blobs or spots on their transparent bodies. We find them difficult to keep and they mostly stay out of sight within the tentacles of an anemone.

There is another small prawn with a transparent body which is occasionally caught off the shores of Singapore in vast quantities. These are much valued for food. We put some into our tanks thinking that they would make good live food for the lion fish and other fairly large specimens. Neither the lion fish nor the others could catch them, however, although they were quite bold little creatures and would seize chopped shrimp from under the very eyes of the fishes. We have seen them worrying very small fishes with the pincers and once one was discovered grazing on an anemone. It was using its pincers to pick up minute particles from the surface of the anemone which had erected some tentacles as if to sting it, but these were only isolated ones – others shrivelled before the prawn. We did not see it actually nip the tentacles though suspect that it may have done so. The writer tested the anemone with his fingers to see whether it felt 'sticky', i.e. still had effective nematocysts. It had, though it was not one of the more vicious kind. The anemone started to close around the finger and in doing so tilted the side on which the prawn was standing. This alarmed the little creature and it started to back away.

When the tilting stopped the prawn continued its journey. It was then deliberately frightened to see what it would do. It left the anemone hurriedly taking the shortest route through the tentacles and not even appearing to try to avoid the outer ones.

We have also kept larger prawns – some of the local ones are very prettily coloured: we had one which was a dark-navy blue with red underside and another which was bright-green. If not too large these creatures add interest to a tank and it is amusing to watch them trying to ease off their shells when they have outgrown them. Really large ones cause too much damage.

Pistol prawns are also interesting to keep. They are very common members of the family Synalpheidae and are found in the intertidal zones often sharing their burrows with the burrowing gobies. They grow up to 2½ inches long and have a claw-bearing leg which makes a cracking sound when the claw is suddenly closed. Hence their popular names 'cracking prawnies' or 'pistol prawns'. The noise is particularly noticeable after the tank has had a good feed of chopped shrimp and is loud enough to frighten one of our Alsatians. This claw-bearing leg is also an excellent tool for shovelling out sand and for erecting a barricade of small stones at the entrance to the burrow. Pistol prawns can sometimes make a nuisance of themselves by removing small corals to use instead of stones, but the moral is to see that they have enough small pebbles. They do an excellent job of scavenging as well as providing amusement and a home for the gobies.

Artemia (Brine Shrimp). We find that this does well if the eggs are hatched in a tank of the green alga which we call 'blanket weed'. If the tank is kept in the open there is no need for aeration. We use this weed with the hatched brine shrimp enmeshed in it to feed our main tanks. Even the non-algae eaters and the corals like this food and it is odd to see fishes so strictly carnivorous as the clowns poking about in the weed. We usually give this food at odd times of the day and not at regular feeding times so that it helps to keep the fishes active and amused. They have this treat once or twice a week depending upon the supply.

14. Echinoderms

In almost all echinoderms the sexes are separate. Fertilization takes place in the sea and most of these animals pass through a larval stage.

Starfishes

Starfishes are found on reefs, reef flats and on muddy or sandy shores, sometimes partly buried in the sand. They move on tube feet which, in most cases, have suckers at the end which enable them to get a grip on slimy surfaces. Their mouths are underneath, facing downwards. The anus is on the top surface of the body. Starfishes have efficient nervous and sensory systems. At the end of each arm is a simple form of eye. Excreta is 'leaked' through various parts of the body in the form of slime.

Oxygen is obtained by taking it in from the water (mostly via the walls of the tube feet and through little papulae or blisters on the body, but some primitive types have special arrangements).

In the wild these animals feed by using the tube feet to force open bivalves and then inserting the stomach. Starfishes do not move quickly as a general rule, but neither are they sedentary and they wander around the tank.

There is a beautiful red species, about 3 to 4 inches in diameter with well-shaped arms, which is occasionally found on the reefs. Another, apparently more rare, has a golden-sand-coloured body with brown markings and this is also very attractive. The drab-coloured *Archaster typicus* is very common locally; this has a greyish or light-fawn body with darker markings and it scarcely shows in the tank.

Linckia, the blue starfish, is not found around Singapore but we have one which came from Java. It is a beautiful Cambridge blue, about 8 inches in diameter, and thrives in our 150-gallon tank, apparently living on algae on the rocks and tank glass. Some species of *Linckia* are a very dark blue and small specimens are most to be desired.

Starfishes with cushion shapes, with warty bodies or with spongy surfaces should be avoided. They do not do well in captivity and if they die may cause disaster. As reported elsewhere, we had a glorious flame-coloured spongy one which died in the night, giving off a detergent-like foam which blanketed the surface of the tank. This caused a lion fish to panic and leap to his death on the floor.

Perfect specimens are seldom found: they usually have at least one arm damaged, but the limb will grow again. A starfish which is rigid is in healthy condition, when sick it will go flabby. They should be handled as little as possible and need plenty of aeration – if this is cut off for any length of time they will die. Some are highly sensitive to changes in salinity and none does well in concrete tanks. We would not try to keep them without plenty of coral rock and sand.

Brittle Stars

Brittle stars are often found in the heart of coral or coral rock. A sponge when broken open may also reveal a nursery full of very small young ones entangled so closely that it is difficult to extricate them.

Like the starfishes, they have the mouth on the underside of the body but there is no anus. Undigested food comes out from the mouth. There are other important differences in anatomy but the most obvious ones are the length of the arms and the smallness of the disc.

Brittle stars have no suckers on their feet; they progress by writhing movements of the arms, pulling and pushing themselves along. Although they mostly come out only at night they are by far the most active of the echinoderms.

We do not have to collect brittle stars – they come in the coral and are always welcome because they are such wonderful scavengers. Also, it is fascinating to see the thin arms waving about at feeding time. The aim seems to be to capture pieces of chopped shrimp without exposing their bodies. (If an arm is attacked it can easily be shed and another will grow.) They can seize food with the arms and then pass it along the underside to the mouth using the tube feet as a conveyor belt.

The colours vary greatly: some local species are beige, purple, green, blue – often with contrasting stripes or other markings.

Brittle stars live indefinitely in a tank. Because of the tendency to shed arms they need careful handling.

148

Gorgonocephalus and *Astrophyton* *(Basket Stars)*

Gorgonocephalus are closely related to the brittle stars, and have a similar anatomy. They come from fairly deep water. We have found them lodged in *Gorgonia* (sea fan) when they were at the 1-inch size. The arms are repeatedly branched and at this size they are attractive. When they grow larger they leave the host and are liable to settle on algae or sponge, stretching out their arms to catch fragments of food at feeding time. After a while they disappear. It is not worthwhile to collect *Gorgonocephalus*, but if you find them in the tank they should be preserved for as long as possible. Large specimens are said to be predatory and are in any case repulsive, being mainly a mass of tangled writhing arms. The only species which we have had have been white, but there are other colours.

Astrophyton are very similar creatures but belong to a different genus.

Sea Urchins

Sea urchins also have the mouth on the underside and tube feet. Unlike the brittle stars they do have an anus, which is on top. The length and texture of the spines vary considerably according to the type of urchin. Some have spines which are almost silky and fur-like, whereas those of others are much thicker and longer and more brittle. The spines are moved by muscles.

A common urchin on local reefs is the black long-spined *Centrechinus setosus*. We kept one in a tank with a *Cerianthus* as contrast and each made a good foil for the other. Sea urchins are difficult to collect because of the risk of breaking the delicate spines, or of causing the creature to shed them. We think that urchins are unsuitable for a community tank and they undoubtedly make maintenance more difficult. In the end we returned ours to the sea. Whilst in the tank it must have fed itself, because it seemed to thrive; presumably it ate algae – it did not seem to damage the coral.

Sea Cucumbers, Sea Gherkins

These tube-like creatures lie lengthwise on the sand and the body often has a much-wrinkled appearance. The mouth is at one end and the anus at the other. They have tube feet but can also crawl about by muscular movements of the body which has both circular and longitudinal muscles to enable it to expand and contract. The skin is slimy or leathery to touch. If lifted and held tail down sea cucumbers may disgorge a small fish (*Carapus*) which often lives inside. Apart from the tube feet which actually act as 'feet' there are others which are arranged like short tentacles around the mouth. These enable the animal to sweep the sand for food. In most cases there are yet other such feet scattered over the body.

Some sea cucumbers can swim by means of elongated tube feet which hang down like the tentacles of a jellyfish; others can burrow under the sand.

Oxygen is obtained by pumping in water (except in one Order which lacks the necessary respiratory apparatus and has to use other means).

Not only are the large sea cucumbers unattractive, they also have unpleasant habits. Some will let out slime to trap an aggressor or anyone trying to pick them up and others can eject the gut which they regenerate later. The object of this manœuvre is not clear unless it is to give their predator something to eat whilst the rest of the animal escapes.

Although we have said that large sea cucumbers are unattractive, even repulsive, the small ones are pretty. They can sometimes be found on reefs flats. Our favourite is an orange-coloured specimen of about 2 inches. We have not been able to identify it and it is no doubt a juvenile form of one of the larger ones.

Sea cucumbers live on organic matter and on algae. They are unsuitable for a tank without sand; the large ones are unsuitable for *any* tank.

Feather Stars

These creatures are related to the stalked sea lilies of the deap sea, which we have not kept. Feather stars are found in shallow water and lose their stalks when quite young: we have never found one still attached to its stalk. The feathery arms are patterned black-and-yellow, black-and-white, green-and-white, brown-and-white or all red and the creatures swim gracefully by the movement of the arms. We do not find them satisfactory in the tank, however, and when the red ones die they give off a red dye which poisons the tank or the collecting bucket.

15. Molluscs

Most members of the phylum Mollusca live in the sea, but the common garden slugs and snails also belong to it. Our main interest is in the molluscs which protect their soft bodies with beautiful shells. These are contained in the following two classes:

Gastropoda

This covers snails with a single shell. These univalves are basically slugs with a shell on top into which the internal organs are packed. Such organs are usually also protected by a mantle. The foot is typically large and fleshy. There is a well-developed head with eyes and sensory tentacles. This class also covers the nudibranchs, which are sea slugs.

Lamellibranchia

This covers the bivalves, which have two shells connected by a hinge. These shells are opened and closed by the action of muscles and the mantle cavity is in the space between them. Mantle lobes project from this cavity. *Tridacna* are particularly well known for the beauty of their frilled iridescent lobes. Bivalves have no head.

Octopuses belong to the class Cephalopoda and are *not* recommended for tank use. There are other classes of molluscs which do not concern us.

The following pages contain short lists of some in which we are interested, showing the family names.

16. Univalves

Conidae (Cone Shells)

These are beautifully marked shells, well known to collectors, but the venom of some species can be fatal to man. Since they are also carnivorous and liable to prey upon other tank creatures, especially at night, we do not use them. If you are proposing to do your own collecting you should first of all learn to recognize these shells (which vary greatly in size) so that you can avoid them.

Cypraeidae (Cowries)

Cowries are very common on tropical shores and on coral reefs and flats. One small red-mouthed species which we have found in Singapore is *Erronea errones*. This frequently browses beneath the rocks. It has three dark-grey transverse bars against a lighter background speckled with brown. The bars and the speckling may be rather indistinct. Shells are usually about 1 inch long. The mantle is dark-grey mottled with black and has many light-coloured small hair-like projections which are very sensitive. We have noticed that cowries will sometimes erect the mantle, at least partly, when browsing, but that it is frequently retracted when they are stationary. It retracts if touched and is obviously more vulnerable than the hard shell. Cowries have eyes in the tips of the long tentacles which they wave in front of them when exploring the rocks. They also have a rasping tongue-like radula which can clean algae off the side of a tank, devour seaweed or, for that matter, cut a hole in our fish nets. At least some are also carnivorous.

A friend in England to whom we sent some *Cypraea arabica* sized about $2\frac{1}{2}$ inches described how he watched them devour a small live pink hydroid, scything it off at the base. First the cowrie opened its jaws and sucked in the top half of the hydroid. Then, having obtained a good grip on it, he swept his radula round the base of the hydroid and neatly beheaded it.

152

We find cowries useful as scavengers because they will eat dead or dying sponge of the encrusting type, dead or dying sea mushrooms and other decaying animal matter. Their own main enemies are shell collectors and they are also a prey to the octopus. The natives of Hawaii are said to use them as octopus bait.

All cowries have highly polished shells; some are speckled like birds' eggs, others have golden circlets. Their sizes vary.

C. tigris – the tiger cowrie – is very beautiful; we kept two of these for some time in our largest tank. (See photograph facing page 160 – the female is the paler of the two.) They were about 3 inches in size and we believed that they had mated in the tank. The female produced a mass of 90–100 egg capsules. These were a mauvish-grey colour, about 2 millimetres wide by 3 millimetres long and they looked not unlike lavender seeds. The male did not take any interest in the laying and hatching of the eggs, which were laid on the side of the glass tank, the mother protecting them with her foot. She had also erected the lower part of her mantle to seal them off completely from intruders. A small shell positioned itself near the eggs and was obviously preparing to feed on the larvae when they hatched. Several times the mother cowrie seemed to be mouthing the eggs and she did not leave them for over three days, by which time the capsules were empty. We never saw any young – no doubt they were devoured in the larval stage.

We have also kept other cowries, including a very large number of *E. errones*. At least one of this species produced small white egg capsules arranged in a rough circle and the mother protected them in the same way as had the larger cowrie.

If you are proposing to keep cowries longer than about 1 inch you will need plenty of sand, coral rock and room for them to move around. They will want algae to eat but will scavenge other food for themselves. The algae growing on rocks and on the glass of the tank should be sufficient for several cowries of the smaller types provided that the tank is well lighted.

Haliotidae (Ear Shells)

These are little whorl-shaped shells, reddish-brown or pinky-brown in colour. There is a line of holes on one side of the shell through which water can escape from the mantle cavity. The mantle itself forms an attractive fringe. These creatures are strictly nocturnal and several of about 1 inch have done well in our outside tanks. It is probable that they need a lot of algal growth on which to feed. The most common local species is *Haliotis ruber clathrata*. A popular oriental delicacy, abalone, comes from the foot of a larger species. At one time the iridescent lining of the shell was used to make pearl buttons.

Olividae (Sea Olives)

Oliva ispidula are the most common local sea olives; they are found in the sand of reef flats, usually just below the level of the lowest spring tides. They mostly lie close to the surface with the snorkel tube – which is pale-coloured and difficult to detect – projecting through the sand. When they move they leave a distinct trail in the sand above them and this often betrays their presence. The process by which they surface and submerge is most fascinating to watch: it is reminiscent of a submarine.

Sea olives are collected in great numbers primarily for the sake of their beautiful shells and they are made into souvenirs in the form of 'bead' curtains, necklaces, etc., which is a shocking waste of these interesting and harmless animals. The shells are usually creamy-white with brown mottling, about 1 inch long. They have a large white fleshy body which seems to be bigger than the shell. In addition to the snorkel tube there are two short stubby feelers which bear rudimentary eyes and above these are thin tentacles. The head is arrow-shaped but is not often seen except when the creatures try to climb the glass wall of the tank. We have never known any to succeed in climbing right to the top because when part of the way up they seek to change direction, the heavy body loses its adhesion and they fall to the sand.

Not only are olives clumsy, they appear to be stupid, too. We watched one on the surface of the sand at the bottom of the tank as it tried to move through a passageway between an anemone and a large rock – all other routes were blocked. The olive made three attempts to find the passage and moved steadily forward each time with the tentacles waving rhythmically until it touched those of an anemone, whereupon it recoiled and submerged. Every time it did this it reappeared at its original starting-point.

The normal food of sea olives is small worms and other little creatures living in the upper surfaces of the sand, but they are also good scavengers and grow to learn that uneaten pieces of shrimp can be picked up from the bottom of the tank. They seem to have an acute sense of smell and will emerge within seconds of food falling on the sand in their vicinity.

154

When they eat, the foot seizes the food morsel and then retracts – spreading out again after the food has been devoured. The tentacles do not touch the food in the process.

We have not known olives to breed in our tanks. If you wish to keep them you will need at least 1 inch depth of sand at the bottom of the tank and plenty of space for them to roam beneath the surface. They are well worth having because they make good scavengers, trace interesting patterns in the sand and are amusing to watch.

Strombidae (Wing Shells)

The largest member of this family which we have tried to keep is the *Lambis lambis* or spider shell. These are relatively hardy. The shell has a whorled body with a large projecting underlip which splays out into seven spines of varying lengths. It can grow to 6 or 7 inches. Juvenile forms have no spines, but as they grow, so the whorl increases, and on attaining near-adult size the overlapping lip projects itself into spines. Thereafter the only growth is in the thickening of the shell. The spines should be handled carefully because they may be brittle. *L. lambis* are found on coral reefs and flats and also on rocky or sandy shores.

These are very active animals with a powerful foot and they stumble around the tank in clumsy lurching movements. Two stalked eyes emerge from channels at one end of the shell and, if the coast is clear, the long, greenish-black, mottled, turtle-like head and neck will emerge to browse on the algae. In contrast to the clumsy foot movements the action of the head has a sinuous grace. In the confined space of a tank, *L. lambis* will sometimes get themselves jammed against the rockwork, unable to reverse. When this happens they must be gently released lest they die of starvation. For this reason, it is necessary to keep a check on their whereabouts.

The top of the shell is usually covered with algal growths, seedling corals or other encrustations and the creatures are hard to distinguish from the adjacent coral rock. Indeed, we had one which looked so much like a rock that a frog fish came and stationed himself upon it. Then a large tiger cowrie came to nibble at the frogfish whom *he* thought was a piece of seaweed. So we had two quite large creatures on top of one fairly small *L. lambis*, which promptly heaved itself up with, considering its handicaps, surprising agility. The underneath of the shell is a creamy-grey colour with mushroom-pink flushing. Some of this colouring shows in live specimens beneath the margin of the projecting lip.

155

L. lambis need a fairly large tank with a good area of sand, coral rock and algal growth. They particularly like the type of green seaweed which grows as a blanket of densely packed fine fibres over certain lagoons. Fortunately this weed is easily propagated.

Trochidae (Top Shells)

Top shells are mostly found on coral reefs and get their common name from the characteristic shape. *Trochus niloticus maximus* is also known as the button shell. Before the development of plastics it was used in the manufacture of pearl buttons. It is a large shell often exceeding 4 inches.

One of our top shells, sized about 2 inches and believed to be *T. gibberula*, had a 'floral decoration' (living *Tubastrea aurea*) on its side. This excited a lot of admiration from visitors and was nicknamed the 'Easter bonnet'. In addition, the shell was prettily marked with pink and red encrusting growths.

Turbinidae (Turban Shells)

We have kept small members of this family which gets its name from the shape of the shell, which is speckled greyish-green with purple and brown markings. It is notable for the large operculum which seals off the entrance to the shell. Children still collect these shells and sell them to the local people who make the operculum ('cat's eye') into costume jewellery and small ornaments. A small live specimen is attractive in a tank. Large ones can grow to more than 2 inches but are not so desirable.

Volutidae (Volutes)

The volutes normally have beautifully marked shells not unlike those of some cones, but larger and more bulbous. They may be anything from 4 to 7 inches long, and will not live in a tank, possibly because they come from rather deep water. A large shell like this, if it dies, may poison a tank.

Order Nudibranchia

Nudibranchs are gastropods which have partly or completely lost their shells: we have occasionally found one with a vestigial shell but in most cases the shells are not apparent. Many have a ruffle of gills on the hind

156

part of the body and may have others as a crest between, or just behind, the two horn-like tentacles at the front. They are often beautifully mottled in purple or orange and there is a white one with black spots. Other colourings are less common, at least around Singapore. We nick-named them 'orchid cows' because the horns are cow-like and the mark-ings remind us of orchids. Some feed on algae but others are carnivorous. The black-and-white type will eat blue sponge until its inside looks blue, as can clearly be seen through the skin. Others eat anemones and yet others corals.

There is a very small burr-like orange or yellow nudibranch which preys upon *Tubastrea aurea*, and is usually found only on that coral. It is a fascinating creature: thin golden papillae are massed all over the top part of the body and they have orange tips. When it wishes to swim it turns over on to its back so that the papillae hang down like tentacles and paddle it along. Progress is not very fast but it seems able to steer itself in the water. If it comes to rest against the tentacles of an anemone these do not seem to worry it. A similar papillated type – but black or dark-brown – preys upon *Dendrophyllia nigrescens*. These are the only burr-like nudibranchs which we have met but we know of at least one other, a grey one, which eats anemones.

The larger species will readily lay masses of eggs in the tank, usually in a whorl of fluted 'ribbons'. We had one which produced a beautiful orange streamer, but the colour of those found in the wild is usually white.

Nudibranchs are hermaphrodite and spend a lot of their time wander-ing around trying to find a mate. When they mate they lay prolifically, exhaust themselves and soon die. For this reason they are not really satisfactory in a tank.

There is one type of nudibranch which should most certainly be avoided. It is large – about 5 inches long, and an unattractive mottled greyish-white. This creature can discharge sepia which is poisonous to some animals.

17. Bivalves

Shells of this type cannot safely be kept with the *Chelmon rostratus*, which will kill them.

Pectinidae (Scallops)

These shells are very well known; not only are they frequently found on rocky shores and reefs, but the outline is familiar because it is associated with a famous trade mark. The most common species are *Chlamys radula* which grows to about 3 inches and *Chlamys transquebaricus* which is slightly smaller. The latter is particularly attractive because of its beautiful red colour. We have kept a *C. radula* and found it hardy. It was amusing to watch as it clapped its way around the tank by opening and shutting the valves. When resting on the bottom with the valves partly open it looks rather like a grinning mouth. The eyes, which are numerous, are in the mantle edge. The mantle itself is inconspicuous.

An attractive small species which we have also kept is *Chlamys madreporarum* which is found among branched coral, especially *Pocillopora damicornis*. This scallop is only about 1 inch long at its largest, but we have found specimens of half an inch.

Tellinidae (Sunset Shells)

Members of this family will burrow deeply under the sand but are said to feed on surface deposits. One of the most beautiful is *Tellina virgata*. It has delicate pink rays on a whitish background. Our specimen was just over 2 inches long and it lived for some time in the tank, though we did not see it burrow. Sand is essential to keep this one. The popular name strictly only applies to *T. virgata*.

Tridacnidae (Clams)

Clams are some of the most beautiful creatures on the reef with their iridescent mantles displayed in the sunlight. Although the shells are themselves lovely in shape, their chief glory is the living mantle – green-and-yellow, brown-and-yellow, purple – dappled with streaks and blotches which look like the reflections of sunbeams deep down among the corals. Small clams will do well in a tank with a plentiful supply of plankton and of light – preferably sunlight. They are scientifically interesting, too, because of the way in which they farm their zooxanthellae, which are contained mostly in the mantles.

We do not recommend keeping clams of more than about 3 inches and they must be watched because if they die they will quickly poison the whole tank.

Class Cephalopoda

This includes the octopuses (Octopodidae). They should not be kept in a communal tank. We had an octopus which grew up in one of ours. We did not discover him until he was about 4 inches long. He must have come in either as an egg or as a very juvenile form and have been hiding among the rocks. Presumably he used to come out at night to catch his prey – certainly we had missed quite a few of our crabs and small cowries for some time before we saw him. In the end he caught and killed our favourite swimming crab and a spider crab which liked seaweed. The only crabs safe from him were two little orange ones living in a piece of *Pocillopora damicornis*. At first we were inclined to leave him in the tank because he was fascinating to watch and all our visitors loved him.

He would come out of his cave and shelter behind a rock, bobbing up and down, just watching us: or glide, ghost-like, over the rocks fading into the background as he changed from almost white through grey and brown to a near black. His tentacles would probe and search all the little holes in the rocks. Like a squid, he could project himself very swiftly through the water, tentacles streaming behind. As he grew larger he learned to give off sepia when approached too closely. (To our surprise this did not seem to affect the other tank creatures.)

After he had caught the two crabs, and one of our favourite fishes, and attacked a small 2-inch shark, we decided to catch him and let him go in the sea, but this was not easy. We tried a method used by the Hawaiians of putting in a dark-coloured bottle, which is supposed to look cavelike, in the hope that he would explore it. A piece of shrimp was added as bait. This disappeared in the night, but he would not enter the bottle whilst we were around. In the end we netted him, but not before he had

159

shed a tentacle in an effort to evade us. We then put him in a large plastic bowl in the fish tank room awaiting return to the sea. Unfortunately, however, he climbed out of the bowl in the night and died on the floor.

The Use of Dead Shells

If you keep hermit crabs you will need a supply of shells of graded sizes so that when they outgrow their present ones a larger home will be available. We do not trust hermit crabs because we think that they are clumsy and destructive, but we would agree that they are amusing to watch when prospecting for a new shell.

Large *Tridacna* shells are valuable as resting-places for anemones.

With these exceptions we do not recommend the use of dead shells because we feel that the available space can better be used for living creatures. It is unwise to buy them from dealers unless you are sure that they have not been chemically cleaned or otherwise 'treated'.

If you decide to use dead shells they must either be thoroughly sterilized by boiling (in a container the surface of which will not corrode in seawater), or they must be collected straight from the beach and thereafter treated as if living (see instructions for collecting rocks and sand). A shell which obviously has decaying matter in it when found should be sterilized, or, preferably, not used.

160

27. Tiger cowries *(Cypraea tigris)*. A 'waggle' fish *(Plectorhincus chaeto-dontoides)* is approaching over the top of the *Goniopora* at centre and a Blue Trigger fish of the *Balistidae* family is also just visible

28. Tube worms, *Turbinaria peltata*, *Tubastrea aurea*, small local green wrasse etc. The greyish, odd shaped coral in the foreground is a *Polyphyllia talpina*.

29. Feather duster tube worms growing out of a species of *Pavona*
    Photograph by the author

30. Alga of the genus
    Caulerpa growing amid
    zoanthids. Note also the
    red filamentous alga and
    the miniature green
    anemone. The coral is
    Turbinaria

18. Segmented Worms

These worms belong to the phylum Annelida. The class in which we are interested are the Polychaeta or bristle worms. Some of them are free-living: swimming, crawling or in some cases burrowing. Others build tubes.

The free-living bristle worms are members of the group Errantia. In appearance they are not dissimilar to the ragworm of European shores, except for the silvery or white bands of bristles on the sides. We have never deliberately collected them, but invariably get some introduced into our tanks with the natural coral rock and the corals which we use. They are excellent scavengers and although in the wild they are predatory we have not known them to cause any problems. Many are luminous. They appear to be mainly nocturnal and will grow to surprising sizes in a tank. These worms readily reproduce themselves both sexually and asexually by budding.

The worms which encase themselves in tubes belong to the group Sedentaria. Members of the Sabellidae family have soft parchment-like tubes with a smooth muddy surface. One of the most common is the so-called feather-duster worm which is frequently found around Singapore. The feathery tentacles are white, flecked and patterned with brown or can be a more sandy colour nearer to ginger or pale yellow. They feed on minor forms of planktonic life and suspended organic matter, conveyed by the cilia on the delicate feathers to the mouth.

They are very hardy in the tank and will live for long periods if un-molested. Trigger fish of the family Monacanthidae and the butterfly fish *Chelmon rostratus* can be annoying to these creatures and so can crabs. All may trim the feathers to a short fringe – either they, or the worms, should be removed before this stage is reached. If pestered too much or if handled roughly the worm can shed its feathered head and grow a new one but it never appears to be quite the same afterwards and will then often dwindle and die.

We like to have a good group of tube worms in our tanks because they are fascinating to watch. If the head is touched or overshadowed they will immediately retract. Some minutes later the feathers will re-emerge with a rotating, sun-burst effect.

Breeding takes place in the tank if conditions are stable enough. The first time this happens it can be alarming. The water may turn a greyish-brown colour as first one tube worm and then another puffs out clouds of 'smoke'. None of the corals or fishes nor any of the other tank inhabitants, however, gets upset by this clouding of the water; in fact, all seem to be brighter than usual and blooming with the sudden influx of new plankton. If this should happen in your tank, do not interfere with the water. It will be clear again within twenty-four hours. Minute tube worms will grow if the tank is free from their natural enemies such as crabs, hydrozoa, trigger fish, etc., and the small worms will form their muddy cases out of the materials available to them in the tank. Their ability to do this seems marvellous to us. Sometimes we have had tube worms grow up in the tank without observing any signs of breeding or even in tanks without adult tube worms and we suspect that occasionally they may come in with rocks or water whilst still very young.

There is another member of this family which is rarer than the others, which we have found on the upper reef flats. This has white feathers in a delicate whorled pattern. Compared with other localities such as Java and Bali, the waters around Singapore are not rich in tube worms. There is a particularly attractive small red species found in Bali which we have brought back to Singapore. It continued to do well here and is still thriving in England.

The Serpulidae family covers similar worms which have calcareous tubes. The most common local species has a delicate splay of white feathery tentacles and a distinct red collar. The tube is an off-white and rather brittle. It should therefore be collected with care because if damaged the chances of the worm's survival are slight. This creature is particularly vulnerable to pecking and is not hardy. We rarely collect it, both for this reason and because of the difficulty of extracting it from the rock undamaged. Although we have occasionally had young specimens of this type grow up in the tank we have never seen any signs of breeding. One specimen which we had was heavily encrusted, in fact wrapped around, with living *Favia*. It looked like a miniature pineapple.

There are other species of serpulids which, although they have calcareous tubes, look quite different because their tentacles are arranged on long spiral lobes and the tentacles themselves are shorter and more bristle-like. Hence the common nickname 'bottle-brush worms'. They look just like the kind of brush with a spiral head with which one would clean out the neck of a bottle. Very small specimens of this type are sometimes found in Singapore waters but the larger and more interesting ones prefer the cleaner waters off the east coast of Malaysia. There they will be found inhabiting living corals such as *Porites*, usually well below the limits of the lowest spring tides. This makes them difficult to collect which is a pity because their varied colours – deep-blue, light-blue, orange-gold and wine-red are wonderful for brightening the tank.

19. Sponges

These belong to the phylum Porifera. There are very many types of sponges from the large basket-shaped ones to minute specimens living within the crevices of coral. It is difficult to think of these organisms as animals, let alone pets, but nevertheless they can add a useful touch of colour to a tank. Sponges are basically very simple animals consisting of a fibrous skeleton and they have aptly been described as animated filters. The body consists of interlacing fibres and it is riddled with small canals connecting up to larger canals (these are the large holes seen in the domestic bath sponge). Food and oxygen are obtained by taking in water through the small pores on the surface of the sponge. The food content is then drained off in flagellated chambers linked to the canal system and waste is ejected with the water flowing through into the large canals.

Sponges are a very elementary form of life and have great powers of regeneration. Small pieces broken off can root and grow and we have had success with pieces (mostly of blue sponge) which have grown from such small fragments. Sometimes sponge has started to grow up in the tank without our deliberately having attempted to propagate it. Any sponge which establishes itself in this way should be allowed to grow up normally; for example, if it grows on coral it should be left alone. Sponge imported into the tank in the crevices of coral is dangerous because it nearly always dies off under tank conditions after a few days, but if the sponge grows up of its own accord after the coral has been in the tank it is usually quite safe. When collecting you should reject any corals with sponges in the crevices or in the hollows inside some of the hump-shaped types. Seaweeds, zoanthids and sea squirts should also be rejected if found embedded in sponge, as they sometimes are.

Sponges should, if possible, be left upon the rock to which they are attached – provided, of course, that they are not growing in crevices or within the body of the coral. Small pieces firmly adhering to the base are best. Even these should be carefully watched lest they rot and contaminate the tank. The first signs of rotting are when the specimen turns a dirty-brown, yellow or grey. Any pieces affected in this way must be removed from the tank and the discoloured portion completely broken off. Unaffected parts can then be replaced, after a good washing in sea water. Smell them first to make sure that you have, in fact, removed all the rottenness. When broken open in this way they will sometimes reveal minute brittle stars, baby crabs or other small creatures which have made their homes inside. Sponges are very unpredictable and so far the only ones which we have found relatively safe are the pink, mauve and blue. These all belong to the class Demospongiae and are non-calcareous. Red, black, brown, grey and turquoise sponges are best avoided.

We had one specimen of pink sponge which grew from 1 inch tall by 1 inch in diameter to nearly 5 inches in height within two months. Even such small sponges are said to process several gallons of water per day.

In the wild, sponges are eaten by nudibranchs and by a few univalves. The small cowrie *Erronea errones* will eat some types of dead sponge, thereby providing a most useful service.

If a healthy piece of sponge suddenly dies in the tank it may be that it has exhausted its food supply. In such a case it is nevertheless essential to check carefully on the rest of the tank inhabitants as it may be that the sponge, being a filter, has suffered first from a spreading contamination in the water or, possibly, from metal poisoning.

Sponges will absorb newly hatched brine shrimp and unhatched brine shrimp eggs if these are scattered near them, but there is no means of knowing whether they appreciate this diet. We think that it is best to leave the sponge alone and let it gain what nourishment it can from the water.

20. Plants and Algae

All animals depend on plants for food, either eaten directly or absorbed second-hand through the flesh of herbivores. The abundance of animal life in the sea is supported by a superabundance of plant life, but more than 99 per cent of this life is in a form invisible to the naked eye. Phytoplankton, the minute drifting plant life of the sea, is plentiful in the upper surfaces of the oceans and depends on sunlight and nutrient salts for survival.

We do not think that it will ever be possible to grow marine plants and algae in the same abundance and with the same ease in an aquarium as it is to grow their freshwater counterparts. A few green algae such as the various species of *Caulerpa* appear to be sufficiently adaptable and some of the silky, hair-like types and some red ones.

Most seaweeds are in fact algae, in that they have holdfasts or handholds instead of roots. Rooted plants are found, but they are less common.

The most successful green marine alga which we have grown is relatively insignificant in appearance, consisting of a thin hair-like growth but when conditions are right it will form dense tangled masses covering rocks or the sides of tanks. For this reason we call it 'blanket weed'.

In addition to being hardy and a valuable oxygenator, it is host to much minute animal life, thus providing a reserve of living food for larger animals. Cowries, *Lambis lambis* and other invertebrates welcome this food and so do a number of fishes – particularly rabbit fish.

Although this weed will grow and multiply under strong artificial lighting it thrives best of all in good tropical sunlight. We cultivate it in outside tanks, primarily for feeding purposes. Initially 'planted' as clumps of floating weed, colonies establish themselves on the sides of the tanks and thereafter cultivation is simple. The outer masses can be harvested and the balance left to propagate a fresh crop. We have found that tanks so filled are ideal breeding grounds for brine shrimps which

166

grow and breed repeatedly, and their little reddish-brown eggs rest in the upper section of the weed.

We have kept only one species of this alga, but there are many similar species which will grow satisfactorily and will not die off seasonally.

Genus Caulerpa

This is a large genus with many (to the non-botanist) apparently unrelated forms. All the types with which we are familiar are green and when thriving propagate themselves rapidly by means of runners. We have found these algae to be relatively sparse in Singapore waters, but in some areas of Java they are fairly prolific and appear to grow most profusely where they are pounded by heavy surf. *Caulerpa* obviously thrives in the turbulent waters of the inter-littoral zone and can tolerate wide variations in conditions over short periods. It is often found in company with heavy populations of small creatures. Most species appear to be seasonal and we have noticed vast patches dying off in the sea. For this reason, when collecting from the wild we do not overload our tanks with *Caulerpa*, particularly at the time when it is dying off naturally in the sea, otherwise the water would rapidly be polluted. All the species are attractive and once established appear to thrive, especially in outside tanks, in the tropics. There, they will even survive the dying-off period and revive to full growth at the new growing time. They do not, however, do well in England. The species with which we are most familiar are:

Caulerpa racemosa. Our own name for this is 'grape seaweed'. When healthy it is light-green in colour with masses of tiny green 'grapes'. Strong runners cling to the rocks or sides of the tank – in the rough waters of its natural habitat this feature must be essential to its survival. Very attractive in appearance, it will thrive with good lighting but is best of all in natural sunshine. *C. racemosa* will not tolerate poor lighting conditions, in which it dies rapidly. In apparently good health one day it can nevertheless be an opaque mass of decaying matter the next.

Caulerpa verticillata. This is one of many similar species – the differences between which are not readily recognized except by the expert. It has a series of fernlike 'leaves' growing from the central stem or from runners. Normally it grows in long strands amongst rocks, securely anchored by its holdfasts, but we have also seen it growing in dense bushy patches – usually on rocks pounded by heavy surf.

167

Because it is considerably less fleshy than *C. racemosa* there is not the same problem if a large mass dies off. Neither does it seem to have such an obvious dying-off season, although undoubtedly there are resting periods. Overall, we have found this species to be more hardy in aquarium conditions, except that it will not tolerate poor light for long.

Caulerpa serrulata. This can be found in much the same conditions as others of the same genus but we have also seen it growing in abundance in saltwater lagoons in Java, cut off from the sea at all but the highest spring tides. This alga is similar to *C. verticillata* but with a more leathery appearance. Although it will thrive in still waters in the wild, we have found it to be less tolerant of aquarium conditions than some other species.

Caulerpa peltata. This is the most delicate of all and one of the most attractive, with masses of little cuplike 'flowers'. It has never lasted in our tanks for more than a few days and cannot, therefore, be recommended.

Genus Halimeda

This calcareous plant remains bright-green in water, but rapidly becomes white when removed. It is a true plant with roots and requires to be anchored in sand or rock. Relatively hardy, it will survive for long periods in the tank but does not appear to grow much in captivity and probably does not contribute significantly to overall tank health. Its main function is decorative.

Red Seaweed

We have never collected this from the wild. Our only specimens came from Indonesia. This seaweed has no obvious roots and grows in densely packed whorls, anchored to projecting pieces of coral. It will thrive and multiply under only average lighting conditions. There is no obvious dying-off or resting period and it can be strongly recommended for decorative purposes.

The foregoing list, though short, covers the few algae and plants which we have been able to grow with any reliability. Experiments with many others have proved disappointing. The attractive, fleshy, green

Codium never survive. Brown algae mostly wither in an indoor tank, but some *Sargassum* and *Padina* will survive and grow in tanks exposed to full tropical sunlight. We had one small piece of *Sargassum* which was introduced into the tank in the heart of a piece of *Symphyllia* coral, which grew to over 12 inches and then died off, floating free in the tank at just about the time when the *Sargassum* in the sea was breaking off and floating away. We deliberately left the broken-off piece in the tank where it disintegrated and disappeared without causing any pollution.

We find it sometimes worth while to leave any *very small* pieces of seaweed found in the heart of a coral. There is another type, small, purplish red, filamentous, which is also sometimes discovered in *Symphyllia* and does well if introduced with that coral.

Despite the poor results to date, we think that ultimately a number of suitable algae will be found to tolerate aquarium conditions and to reproduce themselves in the tank. Those most likely to survive are the green and red algae from the intertidal zone. Plants or algae with large fleshy bodies are the least likely to succeed. Good lighting and reasonable exposure to natural sunlight give the best chances of success in this field.

Until a wider selection of plants and algae becomes available the main functions of plants in 'natural' system tanks will have to be carried out by the invisible phytoplankton and by zooxanthellae (which have been described as 'imprisoned phytoplankton').

21. Adapting the System to Temperate Climates

Previous attempts to introduce the 'natural' system to America from Indonesia do not appear to have achieved the success they deserved. This is probably because the principles were imperfectly understood, even in Indonesia. There is still, indeed, a great deal to be learned. Nevertheless, we believe that the more artificial techniques for keeping marines must in time give place to simpler methods. These are likely to be based largely upon the 'natural' system.

This book lays down some of the guide lines which may enable aquarists everywhere to share the pleasures of the system. We dare to say even now that it WILL work with many creatures, even in temperate climates, if the suggestions made in the present work are thoroughly studied.

Aquarists living in temperate climates who have had some years' experience of keeping freshwater tropicals, should have little difficulty with 'natural' marine tanks. We would like to see these kept not instead of but alongside their freshwater counterparts. Each is the ideal complement of the other.

Although the system is much less complicated than others, and cheaper too, we would not recommend beginners to tropical fish-keeping to start with marines. It is better to gain some experience with freshwater fishes first, especially if you live in a temperate zone. Once a tank is established it is quite safe for it to be left for relatively short periods in the care of the inexpert. We have left ours for several weeks, even months, in charge of office or domestic staff. The important thing is that the minder should be well briefed and conscientious.

We think that a marine tank kept according to the 'natural' system would be an excellent community project for aquarists' clubs and for biology classes in schools.

We have been exceptionally fortunate in that we were introduced to

170

the system by its chief exponent in Djakarta and were later able to draw upon the experience in England of one of the best-known professional aquarists there – one, moreover, who has always in his writing and his lectures (on freshwater tropicals) stressed the paramount importance of keeping as near to nature as possible.

Since 1966 we have been sending occasional small consignments of invertebrates and marine fishes to Mr Derek McInerny. Readers who have visited his aquarium at Ewhurst, in Surrey, may have seen some of these specimens; others will know him through his lectures to aquarists' clubs and through his own book *All About Tropical Fish* (published by Harrap). We are greatly indebted to him for much of the information in this chapter and for the care which he has lavished on the specimens sent to him.

The experimental tanks at Ewhurst are well up to Indonesian standards as far as invertebrates are concerned – even the Indonesians rarely attempt to use live hard corals but rely a good deal upon zoanthids and sea mushrooms, which they regard as 'soft' corals. The fishes not only grow, but mature and display mating behaviour. It is a delight to see them: plump, with shining healthy bodies and bright eyes. Some have become very tame.

There have, of course, been setbacks in introducing the system into England, including some caused by our initial inexperience as packers and one due to the use of an unsuitable tank sealant. This, although recommended for the purpose, turned out to be quite unsuitable for use in saltwater. It killed fishes which had survived at Ewhurst for many months, together with the invertebrates in the same tank.

There have also been losses due to *Oodinium*, but experience shows that once a fish has settled down after the long air journey and is safely past the quarantine period it should live indefinitely, barring accidents.

What can you hope to keep in temperate climates?

No doubt most of the smaller fishes which are commonly imported will prove to be a success. We know that clowns, dascyllus, demoiselles, apogon (*A. nematopterus*), rabbit fishes, gobies, scats and Malayan angels all do well.

We think that eventually, under natural conditions, spawning by such fishes as clowns, dascyllus and gobies will become much more frequent, even in temperate climates, and not the rare occurrence which it is today. The use of living hard corals is not essential to induce spawning. Natural water and a high incidence of dead coral rock are the main factors; sand may assist. Clowns are most unlikely to feel sufficiently at home to breed unless they have anemones. Other invertebrates may also share the breeding tank, but we do not think that they will actually assist the breeding urge. The more mobile specimens such as crabs, shrimps, prawns and possibly cowries may represent a threat to the eggs or newly hatched fry.

Not only do fishes do well at Ewhurst, but so also do many invertebrates. Zoanthids and sea mushrooms and the small green rock anemones will flourish and increase. Larger anemones will survive for many months, although success with these is more variable. Some sent late in 1968 survived the following winter in England and lived till early in December 1969.

There is one invertebrate which has flourished all too well in England. This menace is a hydroid not dissimilar to a freshwater hydra. It may be introduced in large clumps of corals or zoanthids or even amongst weeds. Some of these creatures were unfortunately sent with the earliest consignments exported to England. There they were carefully encouraged and fed individually, until it was realized what a nuisance they had become.

Although these hydroids do not appear to harm even small fishes, too many of them spoil the look of a tank and they make heavy inroads into the zooplankton and other food which should be reserved for more interesting specimens.

Removing them by hand from the craggy corals proves next to impossible and it is even difficult to get them off the seaweeds. Lemon juice has been tried in an effort to kill them, but this destroyed the weed as well. When attached to *red* seaweed, of the type which we have described elsewhere, they can be killed by washing the seaweed in freshwater. This, if done carefully, will not kill it but will get rid of the hydroids.

Scraping them from the glass and sides of the tank will remove a number, but any parts left will regenerate themselves. The electric-charge method sometimes used for freshwater hydra is of course unsuitable for use in saltwater.

We do not have the same problem in Singapore, except in tanks which are kept without fishes. In our community tanks there must be several creatures which prey upon these hydroids and in fact we know that some batfishes will eat them. So also will certain of the larger cowries.

Should you get this menace in your tank, it is worth going to a lot of trouble to stamp it out before it gains too much of a hold.

Crabs do well and grow rapidly but they have hearty appetites and may eat some of your choicer algae and even corals. An exception is the little spider crab which is no trouble. Others of the smaller ones are also harmless.

Pistol prawns thrive, grow large, and can be destructive. Their main fault is that they disrupt the tank by their tunnelling in the sand. We disagree with Mr McInerny over these creatures – he does not think them worth the trouble which they cause. Our view is that they give a lot of amusement, particularly if there is a goby sharing their hole, so we usually have one or two in our larger tanks. But they *can* cause a lot of trouble.

Small 'glass' prawns are hardy and have bred at Ewhurst.

Starfish have also been known to increase and to regenerate limbs.

Tube worms of the feather-duster and bottle-brush type and the small delicate-looking 'sand' ones from Bali do exceptionally well. The large white ones with feathery tentacles and calcareous tubes, which come from Singapore, do not long survive, but they are delicate anyway.

One outstanding success is the red seaweed which we obtained from Indonesia. This is difficult to come by and we had only one small piece so we sent it to Ewhurst in April 1967. It thrived and grew in the tanks there and when we needed some to bring back to Singapore in June 1969 we were able to have some which had been grown in England and which has now increased in our tanks.

The green seaweeds of the genus *Caulerpa* which we have sent back to England have not lived for very long, although they have grown new shoots. We think that most of these are seasonal and that it is uneconomic, at the present time, to try to propagate them in temperate climates.

Sea squirts will thrive and multiply.

Some sponge does well and some has been known to propagate itself in the tanks at Ewhurst, but mostly it is unpredictable and short-lived.

Several hard corals have done well, even breeding, but they dwindle as the sunlight fades, the sand corals being the first to do so. Experiments with new lighting will, we hope, solve the problem, and we are also working on another solution. It is unfortunate that the sand corals, which we find among the hardiest in Singapore, are some of the shortest lived in England.

We advise caution with regard to hard corals. It is obviously good sense to procure your first few specimens in the very late spring or early summer when reasonably good natural light will keep them in peak condition. Any decline is likely to come in late summer or early autumn at the earliest. Given strong artificial lighting of the types recommended, there is a reasonable chance that they may survive to the following summer. Do not be tempted to experiment with ultra-violet light.

Bristle worms are a great success at Ewhurst. They do an excellent job of removing excess food and they grow large and multiply. When we first wrote about these free-living worms (see SEGMENTED WORMS) we did not think much of them, but considered them a handicap to handling the coral. Although we never destroyed anything, we tended to put them back into the sea if we found them whilst collecting. There were always plenty in the tanks, anyway, because when coral rock is lifted they tend to retreat into it and hide there.

However, when we saw them at Ewhurst coming out to feed on grindal worms, we revised our ideas. They are such attractive, active creatures: rather, as we have said, like furry caterpillars, sometimes lightish-red and sometimes golden-yellow, always with silken bristles. Mainly nocturnal they may be, but they do not hesitate to come out in daylight after grindal worm.

Fairly large cowries do well, but the number should be limited as they are algae eaters and will have to compete for the algae which grows up in the tank. Small cowries do not do so well, nor do sea olives. Others of the smaller molluscs have proved very satisfactory, but do not use large-shelled creatures, especially in a small tank.

General advice on applying the system in temperate zones

We have already given guidance as to the choice and setting up of a tank and its maintenance. The same rules hold good for temperate climates, as does the advice on feeding and health. The important point to remember is that it is even more essential to pay strict attention to these matters when you are trying to keep fishes and invertebrates in a climate which is not natural to them. For example, the local seawater, although quite satisfactory, may be poorly supplied with suitable zooplankton; it is therefore particularly advisable to syphon out about one quarter or one third of the water in the tank every three months or so and replace it with new seawater.

Sand from temperate zones is completely satisfactory and the rules which we have given for collecting both water and sand apply as they do abroad. Calcareous rock from local shores could probably be used instead of dead coral rock, but the fishes and invertebrates presumably prefer the latter and it should not be too expensive when shipped dry. Such

174

rock will after a time become populated and will be every bit as good as that collected and supplied to aquaria in the tropics. Once again, no coral cleaned by chemical means should be used.

An interesting sidelight on the use of temperate seawater is that some of the local zooplankton adapts and grows to maturity despite tropical temperatures in the tank. 'Pumpers' – a cold-water form of jellyfish – have grown in the water at Ewhurst and are still thriving after more than eighteen months.

With regard to feeding, aquarists in England are more fortunate than we are in that they can rely upon culturing supplies of grindal worm. Our own fishes, fed mainly on chopped shrimp when in Singapore, will refuse it after they have tasted grindal worm at Ewhurst.

Do not forget that your corals are also animals and not plants: they are essentially carnivorous and require *flesh*, preferably living. The larger, fleshier corals such as *Fungia* or *Euphyllia* will ingest finely chopped pieces of shrimp or other protein. Grindal worm is welcomed by many corals, so is newly hatched brine shrimp. *Tubastrea* in particular responds to the latter food with great enthusiasm. A certain amount of zooplankton will be present in any newly collected water and this will be supplemented by that generated from invertebrates within the tank. Corals very probably also receive a certain amount of nourishment from carbohydrates leaked from their zooxanthellae. Such nourishment, however, will not be adequate for long-term health and starved corals will not survive. The newly hatched brine shrimp, grindal worm, etc., are therefore essential to supplement the restricted food supply.

We have noticed that Mr McInerny feeds most of his specimens individually as well as leaving a surplus of food for the unseen occupants of the tank. Although we have not adopted this practice of separate feeding we have to admit that such care certainly seems to pay dividends in his case.

It may be difficult to grow 'blanket' weed in England, in which event it will be necessary to experiment with other types of green food; but be careful that nothing which may be used in the tank has been grown by any but natural methods. Chemically fertilized greenstuff is best avoided and anything sprayed with insecticide would be fatal.

We have already dealt with THE HEALTH OF THE AQUARIUM. Do not forget that the 'natural' system will not give immunity to infection and diseases – *Oodinium*, in particular, will strike just as hard in a well-matured 'natural' tank as in any other, if you neglect the essential precautions. You will need to be even more scrupulous about

175

quarantine and hygiene generally in temperate climates, where replacement fishes are hard to obtain and expensive. Be careful to ensure, also, that there is no marked change in salinity when introducing local water, and that the temperature is not affected by new water, sand or rock. If you lose seawater through evaporation, top up the loss regularly with tap-water; do not wait until the level has dropped appreciably. Anemones are particularly sensitive to too great an influx of freshwater at one time.

No difficulty appears to have been experienced with *pH* when using water from the south coast of England. This water, which had to be collected at wading depth, i.e., from close inshore, has proved so satisfactory that it is no longer considered necessary to quarantine it before use.

When buying fish in temperate zones make sure that any which have been shipped or stored in artificial seawater are properly re-converted to natural seawater. They should be acclimatized by increasing the quantity of natural seawater in their tank gradually over a period of 7 to 14 days. Preferably persuade your supplier to do this and only buy them after they have survived the acclimatization. Never buy a damaged fish.

Unless prophylactic treatment has been given by the dealer, it may be wise to treat all clowns against *Oodinium*, but this is a point which is perhaps best discussed with him at the time of purchase. Some shippers send their fishes in water which has already been chemically treated and it is worth finding out what treatment has been given before starting your own.

Finally, we come again to the subject of light. Light, above all natural light, is vital to full tank health – you have a whole host of unseen plants from the zooxanthellae within the corals, etc., to the free-floating phytoplankton. This life will give you tanks that bloom generously and water that appears to live. (It is very hard to explain the term 'live water', but the 'life' can be gauged by the clarity of the water above the reefs on a calm sunny evening when the water although crystal clear appears to glow with life and the glow is not entirely from the sun.)

Generous light will give problems with encrusting algae on the front and side glasses. This can be overcome with routine tank maintenance. As we have said elsewhere, we normally leave the back glass and after a number of months the algae becomes quite luxuriant and provides good browsing for resident cowries and other herbivores, including some fishes. Corals, unless they are in poor health, are unlikely to be overgrown by algae. Rocks generally, particularly dead coral rocks, appear

176

to develop a matt type of alga seemingly within the rock, which enhances its natural appearance. We believe that such growth is particularly worth encouraging in temperate climates.

Even in northern climates, overexposure in summer may result in a dark greenish-blue alga almost like slime. Should this develop, remove as much as possible and screen the tank for some of the time to reduce the period of exposure.

In winter, strong lighting will be essential, but this we have covered in our main section on lighting.

Bibliography

General Biology

Animals Without Backbones – Ralph Buchsbaum, The University of Chicago Press 1948, 2nd edition.

An Introduction to Animal Biology – Dale C. Braungart and Rita Buddeke, The C. V. Mosby Co., St Louis 1964, 6th edition.

The Biology of Marine Animals – J. A. Colin Nicol, Pitman, London 1967, 2nd edition.

Dangerous Marine Animals – Bruce W. Halstead, Cornell Maritime Press, Cambridge, Maryland 1959.

Marine Life (The Young Specialist Looks at) – W. de Haas and F. Knorr, Burke Publishing Co., London 1966.

On Malayan Shores – S. H. Chuang, Muwu Shosa, Singapore 1961.

The Sea – Leonard Engel and the editors of *Life*, Time-Life International (Nederland) N. V. 1963.

Fishes

The Fishes – F. D. Ommanney and the editors of *Life*, Time-Life International (Nederland), N. V. 1964.

'Observations on Littoral Fishes of Israel' – L. Fishelson, reprinted from *Israel Journal of Zoology*, Vol. 12, Nos. 1–4, Dec. 1963.

'Observations on the Biology and Behaviour of Red Sea Coral Fishes' – L. Fishelson, reprinted from *Bulletin of the Sea Fish Research Station, Haifa*, No. 37, June 1964.

Fishes of the Marshall and Marianas Islands – Schultz and collaborators, published by U.S. Govt. Printing Office, Washington 1953–66.

The Marine and Fresh Water Fishes of Ceylon – Ian S. R. Munro, published for Department of External Affairs, Canberra 1955.

An Introduction to the Sea Fishes of Malaya – J. S. Scott, issued by the Ministry of Agriculture, Malaya 1959.

Diseases of Fishes – C. van Duijn Jnr, Iliffe Books., London 1967, 2nd edition.

Echinoderms

Echinoderms – David Nicols, Hutchinson University Library, London 1969, revised edition.

179

Corals

Coral Reef Studies – J. Verwey, Proc. 4th Pacific Scientific Congress, Batavia 1931.

Great Barrier Reef Expedition 1928–29 Scientific Reports, published by the Trustees of the British Museum (Natural History).

An Illustrated Key to Malayan Hard Corals – A. G. Searle, The Malayan Nature Society 1956.

Marine Botany

Marine Algae of the Eastern, Tropical & Sub-Tropical Coasts of the Americas – William Randolph Taylor, University of Michigan Press, 1960.

Marine Botany: An Introduction – E. Yale Dawson. Holt, Rinehart and Winston, Inc., New York 1966.

Index

GEORGE ALLEN & UNWIN LTD

Head office:
40 Museum Street, London, W.C.1
Telephone: 01–405 8577

Sales, Distribution and Accounts Departments
Park Lane, Hemel Hempstead, Herts.
Telephone: 0442 3244

Athens: 7 Stadiou Street, Athens 125
Auckland: P.O. Box 36013, Northcote, Auckland 9
Barbados: P.O. Box 222, Bridgetown
Beirut: Deeb Building, Jeanne d'Arc Street
Bombay: 103/5 Fort Street, Bombay 1
Calcutta: 285J Bepin Behari Ganguli Street, Calcutta 12
P.O. Box 2314 Joubert Park, Johannesburg, South Africa
Dacca: Alico Building, 18 Motijheel, Dacca 2
Delhi: B 1/18 Asaf Ali Road, New Delhi 1
Ibadan: P.O. Box 62
Karachi: Karachi Chambers, McLeod Road
Lahore: 22 Falettis' Hotel, Egerton Road
Madras: 2/18 Mount Road, Madras 2
Manila: P.O. Box 157, Quezon City, D-502
Mexico: Liberia Britanica, S.A. Separos Rendor 125, Mexico 4DF
Nairobi: P.O. Box 30583
Ontario: 2330 Midland Avenue, Agincourt
Rio de Janeiro: Caixa Postal 2537-Zc-00
Singapore: 248c-6 Orchard Road, Singapore 9
Sydney: N.S.W.: Bradbury House, 55 York Street
Tokyo: C.P.O. Box 1728, Tokyo 100–91